HOW TO LIVE
LIKE A STOIC

HOW TO LIVE LIKE A STOIC

A Handbook for Happiness

TOM HODGKINSON

BLOOMSBURY
LONDON · OXFORD · NEW YORK · NEW DELHI · SYDNEY

BLOOMSBURY CONTINUUM
Bloomsbury Publishing Plc
50 Bedford Square, London, WC1B 3DP, UK
Bloomsbury Publishing Ireland Limited,
29 Earlsfort Terrace, Dublin 2, D02 AY28, Ireland

BLOOMSBURY, BLOOMSBURY CONTINUUM and the Diana logo
are trademarks of Bloomsbury Publishing Plc

First published in Great Britain 2026

Copyright © Tom Hodgkinson, 2026

All illustrations © Alice Smith, alice-smith.co.uk

Extract from *ME* by Elton John on pp. 154–155 was first published in 2019 by Macmillan, a division of Macmillan Publishers International Limited. Reproduced by permission of Macmillan Publishers International Limited. Copyright © HST Global Limited 2019

Tom Hodgkinson has asserted his right under the Copyright, Designs and Patents Act, 1988, to be identified as Author of this work

For legal purposes the Acknowledgements on p. 204 constitute an extension of this copyright page

All rights reserved. No part of this publication may be: i) reproduced or transmitted in any form, electronic or mechanical, including photocopying, recording or by means of any information storage or retrieval system without prior permission in writing from the publishers; or ii) used or reproduced in any way for the training, development or operation of artificial intelligence (AI) technologies, including generative AI technologies. The rights holders expressly reserve this publication from the text and data mining exception as per Article 4(3) of the Digital Single Market Directive (EU) 2019/790

Bloomsbury Publishing Plc does not have any control over, or responsibility for, any third-party websites referred to or in this book. All internet addresses given in this book were correct at the time of going to press. The author and publisher regret any inconvenience caused if addresses have changed or sites have ceased to exist, but can accept no responsibility for any such changes

A catalogue record for this book is available from the British Library

Library of Congress Cataloguing-in-Publication data has been applied for

ISBN: HB: 978-1-3994-1558-3; EBOOK: 978-1-3994-1557-6; EPDF: 978-1-3994-1554-5

2 4 6 8 10 9 7 5 3 1

Typeset by Lumina Datamatics Ltd
Printed and bound in Great Britain by Clays Ltd, Elcograf S.p.A.

To find out more about our authors and books visit www.bloomsbury.com and sign up for our newsletters.
For product safety related questions contact productsafety@bloomsbury.com

It is the mind that maketh good or ill,
That maketh wretch or happie, rich or poore.
                              SPENSER

BY THE SAME AUTHOR

How to Be Idle
How to Be Free
The Idle Parent
Brave Old World
The Book of Idle Pleasures (with Dan Kieran)
The Ukulele Handbook (with Gavin Pretor-Pinney)
Business for Bohemians
An Idler's Manual
Idle Thoughts: Letters on Good Living

Contents

Dedication ix
Dramatis Personae xi
Preface xiii

1. Seven Stoics 1
2. Socrates 13
3. Love 31
4. Anger 45
5. Education 57
6. Politics 67
7. Pain 77
8. Happiness 87
9. Friendship 97
10. Logic 107
11. Freedom 117
12. Mysticism 125
13. Money 133
14. Fate 143
15. Objections 153
16. Leisure 165
17. Cheerfulness 173

18. Death 179
19. Legacy 189
20. Conclusion 197

Bibliography and Further Reading 200
Glossary of Greek Terms 202
Acknowledgements 204
Index 205

For Henry

Dramatis Personae

Lots of names from olden times are mentioned in this book. It can get quite confusing. Therefore here is a simple ready reckoner to flip back to if you want to remind yourself of who's who. The names are in roughly chronological order. We finish with St Augustine.

Medea: character from Greek myth. She was driven mad by love for Jason.

Sappho: Greek poet and singer who lived on the island of Lesbos and appears to have run a school.

Pythagoras: Pre-Socratic Greek mathematician and philosopher.

Democritus: Greek philosopher who came up with the idea of atoms and influenced Epicurus.

Socrates: Athenian philosopher and the major influence on the Stoics.

Xanthippe: wife of Socrates. Famed for attacking her philosophical husband in the marketplace and pouring a pisspot over his head.

Pericles: Athenian general and de facto ruler of Athens.

Aspasia: consort to Pericles; adviser and friend to Socrates.

Alcibiades: beautiful young Athenian general; mad, bad and dangerous to know.

Diogenes of Sinope: Cynic philosopher who famously lived in an upturned wine cask, dressed in rags and threw away his possessions.

Crates: Athenian Cynic philosopher, teacher to Zeno.

Hipparchia: Cynic philosopher; wife of Crates.

Zeno: founder of the Stoic school.

Cleanthes: second head of Stoic school.

Epicurus: founder of the Epicurean school.

Plato: student of Socrates, founder of the Academy and author of the dialogues.

Aristotle: student of Plato. Founder of the Lyceum. Studied the natural world.

Chrysippus: early head of the Stoic school.

Zenodotus: early Greek Stoic philosopher.

Diogenes of Babylon: early head of the Stoic school.

Cato the Elder: Roman politician and writer. Author of *De Agri Cultura*, a farming textbook. Famed for his austere ways.

Cato the Younger: Roman politician, great grandson of Cato the Elder. Student of the Stoics. Also austere. Wore simple clothes.

Cicero: Roman lawyer and Stoic. Prolific author.

Clodius: enemy of Cicero.

Musonius Rufus: Stoic teacher.

Seneca: wealthy Roman businessman and author of many classic Stoic texts. Also wrote plays.

Nero: Roman emperor and Seneca's boss.

Octavia: first wife of Nero.

Marcia: friend of Seneca. When she lost her daughter, Seneca wrote her a consoling letter.

Ovid: Roman poet.

Lucilius: Seneca's young friend, and the addressee of his Letters.

Epictetus: freed slave who became an important Stoic teacher.

Marcus Aurelius: Roman emperor who wrote a Stoic classic.

Plutarch: Roman historian, author of the *Lives*.

Diogenes Laertius: Roman historian, author of *Lives and Opinions of Eminent Philosophers*, which was written in Greek.

John Cassian: early Christian monk.

Evagrius Ponticus: early Christian hermit and monk who invented the idea of the Seven Deadly Sins.

St Augustine: Christian theologian and fan of the Stoics.

Preface

*They say Zeno was fond of eating green figs
and basking in the sun.*
DIOGENES LAERTIUS

Stoicism was born in the city-state of Athens in 303 BC when a bearded and dishevelled old philosopher spilled a bowl of lentil soup down the legs of an earnest young man of 30. The old man was called Crates the Cynic, and the young man was called Zeno. He was a Phoenician from the city of Citium in Cyprus, an Athenian colony. He'd been shipwrecked near Athens while carrying a cargo of porphyry, a purplish rock used for building monuments. In Athens he found a bookshop (or we might say a scroll-shop) and started reading the *Memorabilia* of Xenophon, a book about Socrates. He was so inspired by the wisdom of the philosopher that he asked the bookseller where on earth he might find men like these today. Crates happened to be ambling past the shop at this moment and the bookseller said, 'Follow that man.'

Crates had himself been taught by Diogenes of Sinope, the notorious Cynic philosopher who was famous for having lived in an upturned wine cask. Zeno followed Crates around and drank in his philosophy, but was a bit too shy, meek and reserved to adopt the shamelessness of the Cynics. These philosophers lived like dogs, hence their name, which means 'dog-like' (compare our 'canine'). They had sex in public, urinated in the street, slept outdoors, refused to work, wore rags, gatecrashed parties, stole wine and spat at the rich people. They were punks. For them, freedom was found in a total rejection of convention. Crates was married to Hipparchia, a well-born young woman who had rejected her smart young suitors in favour of this rather grotty old shambling figure. Imagine Slavoj Žižek but with no clothes on and carrying a stick.

In order to cure Zeno of what he saw as his excessive modesty, Crates gave him a bowl of lentil soup and told him to carry it around the streets of Athens. Later he saw that an embarrassed Zeno was trying to hide the bowl. Crates took his stick and smashed the bowl. Zeno ran away, with lentils pouring down his legs. 'Why run away, my little Phoenician?' shouted Crates after him. 'Nothing terrible has befallen you.'

From this philosophical street brawl has grown the most enduring and popular of the ancient Greek schools. Zeno taught in the Stoa, a cloister in Athens decorated with paintings that one critic has called 'the National Gallery of Athens', which gave the Stoics their name. I guess an equivalent would be teaching in Trafalgar Square. The Stoics were loved by the Romans, who had a Stoic emperor, Marcus Aurelius. They influenced the early Christians like St Paul, and the gospels used terms and ideas they'd developed. They are a constant feature in medieval philosophy. The Renaissance loved them; we find Stoic sentiments in Shakespeare. They remained popular through the centuries into the Victorian and modern eras. Today's American statesmen and soldiers will profess adherence to the Stoic creed. Mental health professionals love it too: cognitive behavioural therapy (CBT) borrows heavily from Stoic ideas.

To be Stoic is commonly understood to mean something like 'uncomplaining in the face of adversity'. Little boys who were beaten at their public schools learned to conceal their tears and develop a stiff upper lip. However, this is a rather narrow view of a complex and wide-ranging philosophical system, which is a lot more hippyish and mystical than it appears.

The so-called 'Serenity Prayer' is a Stoic statement. Stoics have the wisdom to let go of things they can't control, like external events, and direct their energies towards territory they can control, like their reactions to external events. The Beatles' 'Let it Be' is a Stoic song. Stop trying to control external events, man.

As we'll see, the Stoics also believed in a sort of predestination. They believed in fate and destiny. Lives should be lived according to the *logos*, or the way, and it is our duty to 'go with the flow'. When something bad happens, it may not actually be bad, because it may lead to something good. 'I made a prosperous voyage when I suffered a shipwreck,' Zeno would say later of the success of his philosophical system.

The word 'stoic' is even synonymous with 'philosophical'. When something bad happens to someone – say, they lose a lot of money – and they don't complain, we say, 'she was very philosophical about it.' What we really mean is, she was very Stoical.

But there's a lot more to Stoicism than shrugging your shoulders and getting on with it. It has mystical and spiritual components the secularists gloss over, hence its appeal to early Christians. It has all sorts of interesting stuff to say about ethics, morals, grammar, rhetoric, education, love, friendship and the importance of virtue and temperance. In this book we'll go back to the original texts and look at Stoic authors like Seneca, Cicero, Epictetus, Marcus Aurelius and St Augustine. We'll also look at the Stoic influence on Montaigne, Ficino and Tom Wolfe's *A Man in Full*, where Epictetus helps Conrad Hensley cope with a prison stretch.

Cheerfulness is a form of Stoicism. As Epictetus wisely says, 'Don't hope that events will turn out the way you want; welcome events in whichever way they happen: this is the path to peace.'

We'll discover how Stoicism matters today as a living, breathing, practical and rich philosophy which can help us on our route to fulfilment, and which teaches much more than simply holding back the tears. We'll also look at its various legacies, both good and bad. The list is spectacular: Christianity, Indian independence, cognitive behavioural therapy and the 'manosphere' are just four of the many movements that have Stoicism at their root.

I

The Seven Stoics

What can be more precious than to enter into daily communion with the world's wisest people?
TOLSTOY

When we ponder the question of why the Stoics matter, our first task is to ask, who were they? Who invented – and then promoted – the philosophy in the first place?

Here we're focusing on seven Stoic philosophers, two Greek and five Roman, spanning the period 300 BC to 180 AD: that's nearly five centuries. Of course there were and are many, many more Stoic writers. But my Seven Stoics, I think, are the principal, canonical thinkers we need to get to know, and they're the ones I will keep coming back to in this short study.

We'll also mention many other writers, from Christians like St Augustine to the worldly-wise Renaissance dilettante Montaigne, and of course Socrates, who was the original influence on the Stoics. Tolstoy had a distinctly Stoic character. And there are Stoic philosophers working today. Over the last decade Stoicism has enjoyed a major renaissance.

But our Seven Stoics are the most important. They're the Origin Stoics, the ones that St Augustine and Montaigne and Tolstoy read. They are the first and best and provide our essential grounding in Stoic thought.

Doubtless a more intelligent person than me will think this is an outrageous simplification, and that I have been simply criminal in failing to include Cleanthes or Posidonius. Let them carp! I do not rely on external affirmation for my serenity.

FIRST STOIC: ZENO OF CITIUM, 333–261 BC

As is the case with many ancient Greek philosophers, we only know about the work of Zeno, the first Stoic, through report, hearsay and anecdote. Our principal source is the Greek historian Diogenes Laertius, who put together lively accounts of the lives of the 82 main Greek philosophers, beginning with Thales and ending with Epicurus.

Zeno was born in Citium on Cyprus in 336 BC, the same year Alexander the Great became ruler of Macedonia. His father was a businessman, and it was on a voyage with him that Zeno was shipwrecked in Athens.

Zeno, we read, studied under Crates the Cynic, a tramp-like philosopher who had a Cynic wife called Hipparchia, and later launched his own school in the painted market, or Stoa, hence Stoic. Another nickname for his teaching was 'doctrines of the porch', since 'porch' is a translation of *stoa*. He came after Plato and Aristotle. He was tall and swarthy, with thick legs, and was nicknamed 'the Egyptian wine branch'. 'He declined most invitations to dinner,' says Diogenes Laertius. He wrote many books, none of which survive, but their titles give us a flavour of his interests: *Of Emotions*; *Of Duty*; *Of Law*; *Of Signs and Ethics* are a few.

The Athenians said of him that he encouraged habits of temperance and virtue (*arete*) in his pupils.

The story goes that he died after breaking his toe while leaving a lecture. He saw this accident as a sign that it was time to leave the earthly realm and, as he lay on the ground, strangled himself. In other reports he starved himself to death. He was 98.

Diogenes Laertius said that Zeno was physically tough, and embodied many Stoic virtues, including amazing endurance and frugality:

> The cold of winter and ceaseless rain
> Come powerless against him: weak the dart
> Of the fierce summer sun or racking pain
> To bend that iron frame. He stands apart
> Unspoiled by public feast or jollity:
> Patient, unwearied night and day doth he
> Cling to his studies of philosophy.

Sounds a bit prim and puritanical, though, doesn't he, standing apart from the public feast and jollity, thus admonishing the merry-makers?

Zeno was among the very earliest philosophers to talk about the logos or divine reason. When he died the Athenians buried him in the Ceramicus, the area where the potters lived, and which housed a large cemetery.

SECOND STOIC: CHRYSIPPUS, 279–206 BC

Chrysippus was a later head of the Stoic school in Athens. He lived around 280 BC to 206 BC, and therefore was 73 or thereabouts when he died. Again, only a few fragments of his work remain, so we must rely on Diogenes Laertius and comments by later philosophers who may have read his actual books. We're told by Diogenes Laertius that his morals were pretty wild. He endorsed incest and cannibalism:

> In his Republic [*politeia*] he permits marriage with mothers and daughters and sons . . . In the third book of his treatise *On Justice* he permits eating of the corpses of the dead.

In one account, Chrysippus died laughing: a wandering ass ate up all his figs, whereupon he said to an old woman, 'Now give the ass some wine to wash down the figs!' and found his own joke so utterly hilarious that he expired on the spot.

THIRD STOIC: CICERO, 106–43 BC

When it comes to the Roman Stoics we have more original material to consult: dozens of letters, speeches and philosophical tracts by the lawyer, orator and political manoeuvrer Cicero – whose name means 'the chick pea' or 'pulse' or 'lentil' – survive.

Cicero was born in 106 BC at Arpinum in Italy (now Arpino). He was the son of Helvia and a Roman knight. The family also had a villa in Rome. When young, Cicero had three philosophical tutors: there was Phaedrus, an Epicurean; Diodotus, a Stoic; and Philo, head of the Academy. He studied rhetoric and law, as was normal for a high-born Roman male. At 17 he fought in what was called the Social War, a series of battles between the Roman Republic and rebellious provinces like Umbria and Etruria.

At 25 he became a renowned orator and lawyer. His defence speeches became well known, and many survive today. We would not call him a philosopher, exactly, but he was certainly philosophical. He went on a two-year philosophical road trip while in his twenties, studying at Athens, Turkey and Rhodes, where he sat at the feet of Posidonius the Stoic.

In 77 BC he returned to Rome and married Terentia, who, we're told, was rich and had a temper. He had a brilliant public career. In 66 BC he became a praetor, one of the magistrates who governed Rome, and gave more speeches. And in 63 BC he became consul, the highest form of praetor, of which there were only two. His arch enemy Clodius, a Trumpian politician of the day, plotted against him and Cato the Younger, a Stoical senator, advised him to go into exile, which he did in 58 BC, licking his wounds in Thessalonica, before being recalled to Rome a few months later only to find that Clodius had destroyed all his houses. Years of political turmoil followed. When Caesar became emperor, Cicero resigned from politics and turned to writing.

In 46 BC, when Cicero was 61, his daughter Tullia died after giving birth. Grief-stricken, he divorced his second wife Publilia, who'd been jealous of Tullia. He turned to philosophy to console his grieving heart. Then in 44 BC Caesar was assassinated.

Cicero led a number of philosophical discussions with friends at his villa in Tusculum. There was a special hall in this house dedicated to salons, which he called 'the Academy'. He wrote down these conversations, and we can now read them as the *Tusculan Disputations*. He also wrote the brilliantly named *Paradoxa Stoicorum*, meaning 'unconventional ideas of the Stoics', or 'the Stoic ideas which run counter to common opinion' (the word 'paradox' had a slightly different meaning back then). Chapter titles include 'That only what is morally noble is good' and 'That the possession of virtue is sufficient for happiness', both of which are key Stoic precepts: only the morally good can be happy and the virtuous person can remain happy even in terrible circumstances. On the second point he gives the example of Marcus Regulus, a Roman general who was captured by the Carthaginians during the Punic War.

> [T]he tortures of the Carthaginians did not affect his greatness of mind or his dignity or loyalty or constancy or any of his virtues, nor finally his mind itself, for this, defended as it was by so great a retinue of virtues, certainly could not possibly be taken prisoner, although his body was.

Truly we may be free, though clapped in fetters and manacles.

Other books include *De Fato*, On Fate, a discussion of nature and nurture, and *De Finibus Bonorum et Malorum*, On the End Results of Good and Evils, a philosophical dialogue about the Epicureans, Stoics and Academicians. Cicero's plan here was to promote the earlier Greek philosophers to a modern audience. And attack them, too. He writes off the Epicurean theory of atoms as 'a childish fancy' and 'an arbitrary fiction'. In 43 BC, a year after the death of Caesar, Marc Antony sent assassins to kill him. Cicero set sail, but rough winds turned him back. 'Let me die in the country I have often saved,' he apparently said. The assassins hacked off his head and hands and sent them back to Rome, where they were nailed to the *rostra*, the speakers' platform where he'd delivered so many speeches. He was 63. Fulvia, the widow of his enemy Clodius and wife of Marc Antony, thrust a hairpin through his tongue, the sharp, oratorical tongue she felt had caused Clodius so much pain.

FOURTH STOIC: MUSONIUS RUFUS, 30–102 AD

Rufus was born in Volsinii in Italy (now Bolsena), into a knightly family. He was a hugely influential Stoic teacher who taught the better-known Seneca and Epictetus. The early Christian writer Origen cites him as one of the very few people who lived a good life, the others being Socrates, Heracles and Odysseus.

Rufus didn't write much down, but we do have a short bookful of students' notes, taken down by young Lucius, entitled *That One Should Learn to Disdain Hardships*. His work centred around the four Stoic virtues: reason, justice, courage and temperance. He was relatively progressive: one of his lectures argued that women should be taught philosophy. And he had morals, for example attacking men who had sex with their slaves.

FIFTH STOIC: SENECA, 4 BC–65 AD

Born the same year as Jesus, according to some scholars, the Roman aristocrat Lucius Seneca grew up on his father's estate at Córdoba in Spain. When young he was taught by Attalus the Stoic. He became vegetarian and abstained from booze, becoming a water drinker, but his dad, a well-known rhetorician, apparently discouraged this asceticism. He had a political career, and got his foot on the lowest rung of the ladder in Rome by becoming a *quaestor*, a sort of government official or civil servant. He was exiled to Corsica by Claudius over an affair relating to Julia, the sister of Caligula, the details of which remain obscure. He stayed on the island for eight years, during which he wrote books and sent flattering letters to Claudius in the hope of being able to return to Rome.

In 48 AD, the tide turned in his favour when the next empress, Agrippina, brought him back as tutor to her son Nero, who was then 11. He became consul in 57.

But as the years went on, Nero turned against him. Seneca didn't quite live the Stoic brand like the old Greeks, who went around barefoot and wore thin cloaks like the monks and friars (actually, it might be more true to say that monks lived like *them*, but we'll come back to that). He was hugely wealthy, owning numerous villas and slaves. Criticized at the time for his hypocrisy, he declared himself to be a poverty-praising Stoic, but lived in high style. The *Encyclopaedia Britannica*'s 1911 edition puts his net worth at 300 million sesterces, which would be around $400 million today. Famously, he had 500 ivory tables made, each inlaid with citron wood. Quite a dude.

Nevertheless, he wrote excellent philosophical works, and I particularly enjoyed his 124 'Letters on Ethics to Lucilius', which I'll refer to a lot. He wrote philosophical essays, sermons really, on providence, steadfastness, the happy life, anger, leisure, tranquillity, the brevity of life and forgiveness. He's well-known for his tragedies, of which he wrote seven, including *Medea*, and T. S. Eliot commented that 'no author exercised a wider or deeper influence on the Elizabethan form of tragedy than did Seneca.' He's quoted endlessly as 'wise Seneca' in Chaucer's *Tale of Melibee*, and Tolstoy loved him. His end at the age of 69 was extremely messy, as we shall see.

SIXTH STOIC: EPICTETUS, 50–135 AD

The full-time philosopher Epictetus, born in Hierapolis in modern day Turkey, was the son of a slave woman and as a boy was himself a slave. His owner was a freedman and courtier of emperor Nero called Epaphroditus, whose name means 'acquired' in Greek. He was lame, possibly as a result of rheumatism. He took lessons from Musonius Rufus and became a professional philosopher in Rome, giving lectures and seminars to young men in the marketplace like the original Greeks.

Later he set up a school in the city of Nicopolis on the west coast of Greece: the philosophers having been banished from Rome in 90 AD by emperor Domitian, perturbed by the revolutionary vibes of the Stoics, who attacked tyranny in all its forms. Then as now, governments did not always make thinkers welcome. Epictetus stayed in Nicopolis until his death. He was visited there by the more philosophical emperor Hadrian. He lived as a single man, though towards the end of his life he is supposed to have taken in an ailing baby. The earthenware lamp he'd owned became a collector's item.

And like Socrates, and indeed Christ, Epictetus didn't write anything down. His books are compiled from notes taken by his students, and especially one called Flavius Arrianus, who also wrote a biography of Alexander the Great (and wrote in Greek). The books are called the *Diatribes* (or *Discourses*) and the *Enchiridion* or *Handbook*; there are also a few fragments. When I read his stuff I imagine watching a stirring TED talk or attending a lecture by a charismatic teacher at a nineteenth-century public school. Epictetus is one of those aggressive, provocative speakers who loves to do things like calling his pupils 'slaves' and 'idiots'. Of all the Stoics Epictetus is probably the best read today. His words have been reworked again and again in various self-help manuals, and starred in Tom Wolfe's *A Man in Full*. His writings have a distinctively Christian character.

SEVENTH STOIC: MARCUS AURELIUS, 121–180 AD

Our seventh Stoic is the Roman emperor Marcus Aurelius, author of the 40,000-word manual *Marcus Aurelius Antoninus the Emperor: To Himself*, which we now call *Meditations*. This lovely book, which was written in Greek and influenced heavily by Epictetus, is still in print, and amazes the reader with its gentleness, humility and wisdom. How did such a mellow dude get to be emperor of all of Rome?

Marcus Aurelius Antoninus was born in Rome in April 121. His mother, Domitia Calivilla, was a high-ranking noblewoman, and his father, Annius Verus, was a Spaniard who had been consul in Rome three times and died when little Marcus was only three months old. Marcus Aurelius was adopted by his grandfather, Antoninus Pius, who became emperor in 138. Before then, emperor Hadrian took a liking to young Marcus, calling him '*verissimus*', 'most truthful'. He was taught poetry and rhetoric by Herodes Atticus and M. Cornelius Fronto. He became a Stoic philosopher at the age of eight, having met the Stoic teacher Diognetus. He was a serious lad, to be sure: lived abstemiously, worked hard and aimed never to make excuses.

The family had a seaside villa at Lorium, a village west of Rome, which Marcus loved. In 161 Antoninus died and Marcus, along with the other adopted son, Lucius Verus, took over. In this first year Marcus's wife Faustina gave birth to twins, one of whom was the horrific Commodus, who became emperor later and is memorably portrayed by Joaquin Phoenix in Ridley Scott's *Gladiator* (2000).

In Marcus's first years as emperor, disaster followed disaster. The Tiber flooded, resulting in the destruction of fields, the drowning of cattle and then famine. This was followed by earthquakes, fires and plagues of insects, not to mention trouble in Britain, where the soldiers campaigned for their general, Statius Prisicius, to declare himself emperor. Marcus went to war with various tribes, and in 169 the useless Verus thankfully died (there were rumours that Marcus had poisoned him).

There followed good years. One biographer, F. W. Farrar, described Marcus as the very model of a modern Roman emperor, listing some of his achievements and adding that they kept him in 'severe labour' from early in the morning till after midnight:

> the registry of the citizens, the suppression of litigation, the elevation of public morals, the care of minors, the retrenchment of public expenses, the limitation of gladiatorial games and shows, the care of roads . . . even the regulation of street traffic.

Marcus Aurelius apparently went to the games and shows, but used the time to read books and make notes, and his political achievements improved the lot of slaves, women and children.

In 169 there was more fighting with German tribes, including the Vandals, the Quadi, the Marcomanni and the Sarmatians. In 174 Marcus achieved victory over the Quadi, aided by a sudden storm which some saw as a miracle.

Marcus was in Germany in 175 when he heard that the governor of Asia, Avidius Cassius, had declared himself emperor. Cassius was duly assassinated, and his head was brought to Marcus, who persuaded the Senate to pardon

Cassius's family. His wife Faustina, who had borne 11 children (and was said to have been serially unfaithful), died in 176.

On a visit to Athens, Marcus was initiated into the Eleusinian mysteries. This was a sort of mystical well-being retreat that was popular at the time. As its name suggests, what actually happened there remains obscure, though some accounts say that fasting and bathing were involved. This experience gave him the idea of starting philosophical schools across the Roman empire, and he endowed chairs in rhetoric and philosophy.

He was not a fan of the Christians, and in 177 is supposed to have persecuted them.

Marcus was fighting the Germans again when he died, either in Lower Pannonia (now Serbia) or in Vindobona (now Vienna), after seven days of illness. Some accounts say he was poisoned by Commodus (the theory gleefully taken up in *Gladiator*). The other, more likely, theory is that he died of chronic stomach disease. The date was 17 March 180, and he was just 59.

John Stuart Mill described Marcus's *Meditations* as almost equal to the Sermon on the Mount, high praise indeed. Tolstoy was also a fan and quoted him non-stop; he agreed with the Stoics that we all need to put more work into the development and care of our souls.

So there are the Seven Stoics.

But before they were even born, there was another man, whom we could call the founding father of their philosophy. His name was Socrates.

Socrates

Ye have slain, have slain, the all-wise, the innocent,
the Muses' nightingale.

EURIPIDES

In the beginning was Socrates. To understand the Stoics we need to understand this brilliant and often confusing figure. He was their source, their inspiration, the man without whom none of it would have happened. Stoic writers continually refer to Socrates as a model for virtuous behaviour.

Socrates was, in many ways, Christ-like. He did not work, he wrote nothing down, he went around without shoes, lived in poverty, talked about carpenters and was executed by the state. Yet he was more worldly than Christ. He had sex with men and women. He drank wine all night; he played the lyre; he had three sons; he fought in the war against the Spartans when young; he danced and partied; he wrestled, got into fights, rowed with his wife.

What we know of him was recorded by two younger contemporaries, Plato and Xenophon, and preserved in anecdotes by later writers like Diogenes Laertius and

Plutarch. These anecdotes formed the basis of much Stoic teaching. The Stoics would have known everything about the life of Socrates, from his birth in 469 BC, his boyhood in the bustling new democratic city state, his youth as a soldier, his strange relationship with the beautiful young general Alcibiades, his rocky marriage, his middle age as a famous philosopher, fatherhood, late middle age as an irritant to the state to, finally, his trial and subsequent execution in 399 BC at the age of 70, following an electrifying court case.

Socrates was a citizen of Athens, and it might help to paint a quick portrait of this successful city as it was then. The population is around 100,000. There are around 40,000 so-called free men, and the rest of the population is comprised of women, slaves and children. Athens is an independent, self-governing state, and has grown rich thanks to its silver mines in a region called Laurium, about 50km south of Athens. The silver, mined mainly by slaves, is used to make beautiful coins that feature the goddess Athena on one side and a large-eyed owl on the other. Money is being poured into public buildings. Everywhere the stonemasons and sculptors are at work. The great temple to Athena, the Parthenon, is yet to be built, but there are plenty of temples, outdoor theatres and magnificent aqueducts.

Athens is one of around 1,000 city states in Greece. It's a system that was copied in medieval Europe, and to get an idea of what Athens felt like you could do worse than visit somewhere like Florence or Arezzo which, although today clearly part of the modern nation we call Italy, retain some of the character of the period when each city looked after its own affairs, had its own distinct personality and economy, and worked in competition or cooperation with other city states. Streets were narrow and filled with lots of people wandering around and talking, talking, talking. Plus horses and donkeys, the original low-carbon forms of transport.

And the Athenians are in the process of inventing democracy, or a version of it. In Greek, *demos* means 'the people', and *kratos* means 'power'. Hence 'people power'. There is no king or queen or president or tyrant. The people – or at least some of them – decide together how things should be run.

It's an intensely participative democracy. Unlike our version, where we elect representatives, the free men of Athens are intimately involved in its everyday affairs, and there are endless assemblies, meetings, councils and gatherings of jurors. Women, children, slaves and foreign residents don't get to vote. There are three councils. The Assembly, called *ekklesia*, meets every ten days or so and is attended by five or six thousand Athenian voters. They meet at an outdoor space called the Pnyx and vote by sticking their hands in the air. The votes are counted by a team of court functionaries.

There's also the Council of 500 or Boule. Five hundred men are selected at random from the list of free men in Athens. For a year, they comprise an enormous jury which meets most days to debate and vote on issues of the day.

Outside each court stands a strange machine, shaped something like a tall bookcase made of stone. It's called a *kleroterion,* and was designed to select jurors at random just before the case started and therefore avoid attempts at bribery. Name tags of citizens are inserted into slots. A crank on the side of the machine is turned by an official and randomly produces a black or white ball. A white ball means the juror has been selected for that day's proceedings. Black means he's been excluded.

Then there's the *dikasteria* or Dicastery. This is where citizens of Athens brought court cases against each other, and again there were 500 jurors, called Dicasts, chosen at random each day. There are no middlemen like lawyers or police in ancient Athens: the accusations and the defence are all conducted by the people themselves.

The city is also intensely religious. There are shrines and temples everywhere, and some pretty weird customs. People like Socrates' dad worked on making sculptures called *hermae*, which were dotted around the city. These featured a man's head on top of a plain block of stone, with a set of genitalia protruding from the lower half (you'll have to see a picture). There were household gods and animal sacrifice.

Priestesses too. Just over 100 miles to the north of Athens was the city of Delphi. This was home to a number of temples, and where the famous inscription 'Know thyself' was carved. At the back of one of these temples sat a woman on a three-legged stool attended by priests. Called the *Pythia*, meaning something like 'the informed one', she was the original agony aunt. From beneath her, mind-bending gases emerged from the underworld. She was the oracle, a priestess, and would utter odd riddles when asked questions. (In return the questioner would have to sacrifice a goat.)

So this is the Athens of Socrates. He was born as a member of the Alopece district, whose members were part of the Antiochis, one of ten 'tribes' or districts, or *phylai* in Athens, something like the *contrade* of today's Italian cities. His father was a sculptor called Sophroniscus, and his mother a midwife called Phaenarete. From early childhood Socrates exhibited eccentric behaviour. He was not like other boys. He had a habit of going into long trances. This worried his parents. Later he said that he was constantly accompanied by a *daimon*, a divine spirit that spoke to him. This *daimon* would not give him positive advice, only negative. If he heard no inner voice telling him to stop doing what he was doing, he assumed he could carry on.

Socrates' *daimon* was something like a conscience. At his trial, of which more later, Socrates said to the 501 assembled jurors,

> A voice is present with me – a certain agency of God, somewhat divine . . . Now this began with me from my childhood; a certain voice which always, when it comes, turns me aside from that which I am about to do, but never impels me to do anything.

The voice, he says, told him not to become a politician. 'It is this which opposed my mixing in politics, and I think very wisely.'

The *daimon* is important to our understanding of Stoicism. Conscience literally means 'knowledge of oneself', and of course has evolved to mean something like 'a sense of personal reality', according to the OED. It was Socrates' sense of morality and the virtuous that told him, for example, to avoid politics. This idea of conscience will appear later in Stoic thought, and indeed in early Christian thought. It also reveals a mystical, Blakeian side to Socrates, often missed by his rational fans.

Stoics, as we'll see, admire resilience, toughness and fortitude, again qualities we see demonstrated in the life of Socrates. As a young soldier in the Peloponnesian wars with Sparta he was renowned for his sturdiness and stamina – walking barefoot in the snow, for example. He distinguished himself in battle by rescuing his mess mate, the beautiful young aristocrat Alcibiades, who was to develop an enormous crush on him.

His frenemy, the comic playwright Aristophanes, who teased him in his play *The Clouds*, also admired Socrates' fortitude. 'Never art thou weary,' he wrote, 'whether standing or walking, never numb with cold, never hungry for breakfast; from wine and from gross feeding and all other frivolities thou dost turn away.' Yes, that's a slightly old-fashioned translation, but you get the gist.

In middle age Socrates became a philosopher. He would sit around in the marketplace and argue with everyone about everything. And he really annoyed people – roused them to physical violence. But he accepted all attacks on him with remarkable equanimity. 'Owing to his vehemence in argument', says Diogenes Laertius,

> men set upon him with their fists or tore his hair out; and . . . for the most part he was despised and laughed at, yet bore all this ill-usage patiently. So much so that, when he had been kicked, and someone expressed surprise at his taking it so quietly, Socrates rejoined, 'Should I have taken the law of a donkey, supposing that he had kicked me?'

The philosopher dealt calmly with written attacks, too. The writers of the day, the poets and the dramatists, were constantly slinging mud at one another. But Socrates didn't care. In fact, very wisely, he thought that maybe sometimes the haters might have a point. 'We ought not to object', he used to say, 'to be subjects for the Comic poets, for if they satirize our faults they will do us good, and if not they do not touch us.'

Socrates was also even-tempered with his wife, Xanthippe. Doubtless he was extremely annoying to live with – after all, he never earned any money and loved arguing. And when he irritated Xanthippe she certainly didn't hold back. According to one story, when he returned home at dawn after a drinking session with his mates she poured a pot of water over his head. This scene has been commemorated in more than one nineteenth-century painting. In some tellings the water pot became a piss-pot. Neither did she appreciate it when Socrates did an 'all back to mine'. According to Plutarch, she once got quite violent.

> After Socrates brought Euthydemos home from the Palaestra, Xanthippe assailed them with rage, gave them a tongue-lashing and flipped over the table. Euthydemos rose and was leaving, beset by anger himself.

Socrates, though, reacted with his characteristic detachment and humour. 'Didn't a bird fly in and do the same thing yesterday at your house? We weren't put out then!'

On another occasion, Socrates was teaching – for free as usual – in the marketplace. Perhaps he was asking a group of young men to define 'democracy', or ask them what love meant, or how to manage a household efficiently. He delighted in making his pupils question their received opinions. Suddenly Xanthippe appeared, ran across to her husband and tore off his cloak.

Socrates' friends suggested he fight back, but he resisted becoming a public spectacle. 'Sure, that way when we are punching each other, each of you can root, "Well hit, Socrates!" and "Well done, Xanthippe!"'

Once he brought home a seed cake that had been given to him as a present by his young friend, the beautiful general Alcibiades. In a fit of jealousy Xanthippe threw it on the ground and stamped on it. A Roman writer, Aulus Gellius, said that Socrates learned equanimity from Xanthippe.

> Alcibiades asked Socrates why he didn't kick his rather bitter wife out of the house. Socrates said, 'Because, when I put up with her at home, such as she is, I develop a tolerance from the exercise, which allows me to bear a bit more lightly the insults and injustices of the outside world.' He said he saw Xanthippe as a racehorse: her strong will taught him how to handle others. 'Accustomed to Xanthippe, I have it easy with the rest of humanity.'

Of course, Xanthippe may have had good reason to get annoyed with Socrates. After all, he earned no money and spent his time at the gymnasium or in the streets, philosophizing endlessly with his young male admirers. But actually I think these stories demonstrate Socrates' humanity. We don't often hear much about the domestic life of the philosopher. That Socrates had a turbulent time as a husband makes him 'relatable' to his fans. He is flawed. And we can also be inspired by his proto-Stoicism in the face of domestics. He maintains an almost mystical detachment from worldly concerns. He can laugh at the problems of daily life, yet he does not flee them. He always looks on the bright side of life.

Our Socratic tales also attest to Socrates' embrace of simple living and frugality, another key Stoic virtue. Diogenes Laertius offers us this nice little nugget.

> Alcibiades once offered him a large site on which to build a house; but he replied, 'Suppose, then, I wanted shoes and you offered me a whole hide to make a pair with, would it not be ridiculous for me to take it?'

And there's the well-known Socratic statement of anti-consumerism: 'Often when he looked at the multitude of wares exposed for sale, he would say to himself, "How many things I can do without!"' For Socrates, it was godlike to do little and want little, says Diogenes Laertius:

> He used to say that he most enjoyed the food which was least in need of condiment, and the drink which made him feel the least hankering for some other drink; and that he was nearest to the gods in that he had the fewest wants.

As for sex, he demonstrated amazing restraint. We should point out that sex and sexuality were very different in ancient Greece. In some respects, Athens was more liberal. Older married men were often bisexual: they would have younger boyfriends with whom they had some sort of sexual relationship. There was no sense of 'gay' or 'straight' – everyone, it seemed, was polysexual, non-binary. There were older male couples. Women had girlfriends. Men had mistresses who might have a lot of power. For example, the military top man of

Athens, Pericles, had a mistress called Aspasia who was an important figure politically. There were prostitutes and there were the high-class courtesans, the *hetairai*. These were Nell Gwynn types: well-educated and witty, they lived alone or in groups and enjoyed an enviable degree of independence. They could earn a lot, too. The fourth-century Athenian *hetaira* Phrynne became so rich that she offered to pay for the rebuilding of the walls of Thebes.

Socrates demonstrated his powers of self-control by, famously, resisting the advances of Alcibiades. Now this Alcibiades was by far the most fancied man in Athens. Imagine Timothy Chalamet crossed with Bill Clinton and you might get close to a notion of his appeal. He was young, beautiful, rich and an accomplished soldier. Socrates was old – or oldish – balding, poor, bearded and ugly, with bulging eyes.

Alcibiades decided he was going to seduce the older philosopher. He tried three times, and three times he was rebuffed. The first time, according to Plato's *Symposium*, Alcibiades went to visit Socrates and sent his servant away so they could be alone together.

> Now I fancied that he was seriously enamoured of my beauty . . . for I had a wonderful opinion of the attractions of my youth . . . Well, he and I were alone together, and I thought that when there was nobody with us, I should hear him speak the language which lovers use to their loves when they are by themselves, and I'd be delighted. Nothing of the sort; he conversed as usual, and spent the day with me and then went away.

The second time, Alcibiades reckoned that a spot of naked wrestling, very popular in Athens, might do the trick.

> Afterwards I challenged him to the palaestra; and he wrestled and closed with me several times when there was no-one present; I fancied that I might succeed in this manner. Not a bit; I made no way with him.

Finally he entertained Socrates at home. The wine was poured, and the two men ate while reclining on a couch. All seemed to be going according to plan.

> After we had supped, I went on conversing far into the night, and when he wanted to go away, I pretended that the hour was late and that he had much better remain. So he lay down on the couch next to me, the same on which he had supped, and there was no-one but ourselves sleeping in the apartment.

The frustrated, excited and desperate Alcibiades then decided that the time for subtle innuendo was over.

> When the lamp was put out and the servants had gone away, I thought that I must be plain with him and have no more ambiguity. So I gave him a shake, and I said: 'Socrates, are you asleep?'
> 'No', he said.
> 'Do you know what I am meditating?'
> 'What are you meditating?' he said.
> 'I think', I replied, 'that of all the lovers whom I have ever had you are the only one who is worthy of me, and you appear to be too modest to speak.

> Now I feel that I should be a fool to refuse you this or any other favour, and therefore I come to lay at your feet all that I have and all that my friends have, in the hope that you will assist me in the way of virtue, which I desire above all things, and in which I believe that you can help me better than anyone else.'

After a bit of chit-chat, Alcibiades believed he had at last succeeded (note the detail about Socrates' threadbare cloak which he wears even in the depths of winter).

> I fancied that he was smitten, and that the words which I had uttered like arrows had wounded him, and so without waiting to hear more I got up, and throwing my coat about him crept under his threadbare cloak, as the time of year was winter, and there I lay during the whole night having this wonderful monster in my arms. This again, Socrates, will not be denied by you. And yet, notwithstanding all, he was so superior to my solicitations, so contemptuous and derisive and disdainful of my beauty . . . nothing more happened, but in the morning when I awoke (let all the gods and goddesses be my witnesses) I arose as from the couch of a father or an elder brother.

On another occasion, the 'wonderful monster' supposedly barged into a *heitarai*'s house when Alcibiades was visiting her, to tell the young sex-god off for indulging his appetites in such wanton fashion. This scene has inspired a number of raunchy paintings featuring exposed breasts with titles like *Socrates Rebukes Alcibiades in the House of the Courtesans*.

This sort of behaviour got Socrates the reputation of being wise, which clearly reached the priestess at Delphi. One day his friend, the crow-like Chaerophon, took the 100-mile trip to Delphi to consult the oracle. Having bought and sacrificed a goat, he waited his turn to consult with the Pythia. When his turn came (as Socrates would declare at his trial), 'He asked the oracle to tell him whether anyone was wiser than I was, and the Pythian prophetess answered, that there was no man wiser.'

Perhaps Socrates' most stunning and dramatic act of Stoicism was his cheerfulness when faced with death. When he was 70 he was put on trial by former allies. This was the accusation:

> This indictment and affidavit is sworn by Meletus, the son of Meletus of Pitthos, against Socrates, the son of Sophroniscus of Alopece: Socrates is guilty of refusing to recognize the gods recognized by the state, and of introducing other new divinities. He is also guilty of corrupting the youth. The penalty demanded is death.

There were two other accusers, Anytus and Lycon. Anytus may have been motivated partly by the fact that Socrates was rumoured to have had a fling with his son.

Socrates went up in front of 501 jurors. In his defence, which lasted three hours and was recorded by both Plato and Xenophon in accounts they called *The Apology* (but should have been called *The Non-Apology*), he explains that he has been trying to follow God who, he reckons, had told him to be a philosopher. And he says people should spend less time earning money and more time looking after their souls.

> I shall obey God rather than you, and while I have life and strength I shall never cease from the practice and teaching of philosophy, exhorting anyone whom I meet and saying to him after my manner: You, my friend, – a citizen of the great and mighty and wise city of Athens, – are you not ashamed of heaping up the greatest amount of money and honour and reputation, and caring so little about wisdom and truth and the greatest improvement of the soul, which you never regard or heed at all?

He goes on to assert that he has done the city a great service.

> For I do nothing but go about persuading you all, old and young alike, not to take thought for your persons or your properties, but first and chiefly to care about the greatest improvement of the soul. I tell you that virtue is not given by money, but that from virtue comes money and every other good of man, public as well as private . . . I am that gadfly which God has attached to the state, and all day long and in all places am always fastening upon you, arousing and persuading and reproaching you.

Socrates made no attempt whatsoever to apologize. By 280 to 221 the jurors voted 'guilty'. The law said that defendants were allowed to suggest their own punishment, and Socrates outraged the jurors first by saying he should pay a risible fine, and then by suggesting he be given free meals. 'What would be a reward suitable to a poor man who is your benefactor, and who desires leisure that he may instruct you? There can be no reward so fitting as maintenance in the Prytaneum.'

Once condemned, Socrates looks on the bright side of death.

> There is great reason to hope that death is a good; for one of two things – either death is a state of nothingness and utter unconsciousness, or, as men say, there is a change and migration of the soul from this world to another. Now if you suppose that there is no consciousness, but a sleep like the sleep of him who is undisturbed even by dreams, death will be an unspeakable gain . . . But if death is the journey to another place, and there, as men say, all the dead abide, what good, O my friends and judges, can be greater than this?

Socrates was clapped in irons. Then, as a result of a strange confluence of events to do with religious festivals and boats, his execution was delayed by four weeks. He spent this time in prison, taking visits from friends, and chatting.

On one occasion his jailor removed the fetters from his ankles. Again Socrates manages to look on the bright side, with some philosophizing about pleasure and pain.

> Socrates sat up on the bed [writes Plato], bent his leg and rubbed it with his hand, and as he rubbed he said, 'What a strange thing that which men call pleasure seems to be, and how astonishing the relation it has with what is thought to be its opposite, namely pain! A man cannot have both at the same time. Yet if he pursues and catches the one, he is almost always bound to catch the other also, like two creatures with one head . . . This seems to be happening to me.

My bonds caused pain in my leg, and now pleasure seems to be following.'

His friends offered to help him escape, but he chose to face his fate with *ataraxia* or tranquillity. As Plutarch put it, 'He would not yield to their entreaties, nor withdraw from death, but maintained an inflexible mind in the last extremity.'

Socrates' friends asked him how on earth he could remain so cheerful in the face of certain death. Well, he replied,

> He who has lived as a true philosopher has reason to be of good cheer when he is about to die, and that after death he may hope to receive the greatest good in the other world . . . why, having had the desire of death all his life long, should he repine at the arrival of that which he has been always pursuing and desiring?

As Socrates has spent his life trying to become a soul-conscious person, he says he's going to be happy to be rid of his troublesome body.

> For the body is a source of endless trouble to us by reason of the mere requirement of food; and also is liable to diseases which overtake and impede us in the search after truth: and by filling us so full of loves, and lusts, and fears, and fancies, and idols, and every sort of folly, prevents our ever having, as people say, so much as a thought. For whence come wars, and fightings, and factions? whence but from the body and the lusts of the body? For wars are occasioned by the love of money, and money has to be acquired

> for the sake and in the service of the body; and in consequence of all these things the time which ought to be given to philosophy is lost.

Finally, he says that swans spend their last day on earth singing more lustily than ever, even though they know they are going to die.

> And I, too, believing myself to be the consecrated servant of the same God, and the fellow servant of the swans, and thinking that I have received from my master gifts of prophecy which are not inferior to theirs, would not go out of life less merrily than the swans.

Socrates took the hemlock from a stone vial handed to him by the executioner. His friends started sobbing. 'What are you all doing?' he rebuked them.

> I am so surprised at you. I had sent away the women mainly because I did not want them to lose control in this way. You see, I have heard that a man should come to his end in a way that calls for measured speaking. So, you must have composure, and you must endure.

The hemlock gradually paralysed his body from the feet upwards, and Socrates died. His last words are said to be, 'Don't forget to sacrifice a rooster to Asklepios.' Readers have puzzled over these words. But as Asklepios was the god of healing, they're often taken to mean that Socrates was encouraging his followers to continue his work by engaging in argument, or *logos*, which is often translated as 'the word'. Certainly earlier in this dialogue he tells his friend Phaedo to keep the *logos* alive.

It didn't take long for the Athenians to realize they'd made a terrible error. 'The Athenians felt such remorse that they shut up the training grounds and gymnasia,' writes Diogenes Laertius. 'They banished the other accusers but put Meletus to death; they honoured Socrates with a bronze statue, the work of Lysippus, which they placed in the hall of processions.'

Then philosophical schools started to appear, each one influenced by the master's example, and each seeking to distil his life and teachings into a set of principles or at least attitudes. There were the Cynics, who lived without possessions, spat at the rich and abhorred convention; the Sceptics, who accepted they knew nothing and asked questions; Plato's Academics, who studied truth, beauty and the higher things; the Aristotelians, who counselled reason, study and the middle path; the Epicureans, who lived in communes and were materialists who avoided pain; and of course, the most popular and enduring of them all, the Stoics. Let's see what they have to say about that most unnerving of passions, love.

3

Love

> *The only thing I say I know is the art of love.*
> SOCRATES
>
> *This fellow is wracked by love for another man's wife; that one with love for his own.*
> SENECA

The Greeks, as you may well know, identified different kinds of love. They had *philia* or deep friendship, hence philosophy or 'the love of wisdom'. There was *agape*, or selfless love for the world, and *mania*, meaning obsessive love.

What we're interested in here is *eros*: romantic love, sexual love, passionate love. That impish sprite, one of the passions, a god, was causing havoc right from the beginning. The great and grand old poet Hesiod, writing pretty early on in our story, in the seventh century BC, gives us the first mention of *Eros* in his long poem *Theogony*. In this origin story, Eros is the son of Chaos, the first ever god. Seems that Eros was very good-looking and had special powers. Hesiod writes:

> In truth at first Chaos came to be, but next wide-bosomed Earth, the ever-sure foundation of all

the deathless ones who hold the peaks of snowy
Olympus, and dim Tartarus in the depth of the wide-
pathed Earth, and Eros, fairest among the deathless
gods, who unnerves the limbs and overcomes the
mind and wise counsels of all gods and all men
within them.

For the singer and poet Sappho, writing around 600 BC, Eros was highly dangerous to know. In her telling, he is the son of Aphrodite, the goddess of love. From what we know (which is not much), poor Sappho was tormented by Eros. She desired both men and women in obsessive fashion. The word 'lesbian' is of course derived from her island home Lesbos. In one account she ran a poetry school on Lesbos, and she certainly became almost as famous and respected as Homer.

We imagine Sappho reclining with other nymphs, all pouring sweet nectar into one another's mouths. During one of her sessions of sitting around doing nothing with the other Lesbians, Eros pounces, as described in the following Sapphic lyric. The words were designed to be accompanied by the lyre, which Sappho would play. It is also said that she invented the plectrum. So let us imagine her singing this lament to her companions, Atthis, Telesippa and Megara:

My dreaming eyes saw Eros from afar
    Coming from heaven in his mother's car,
In purple tunic clad; and at my heart
    The God was aiming his relentless dart.
    He whom fair Aphrodite called her son,
    She, the adored, she, the imperial One;
He passed as winds that shake the soul, as pains

> Sweet to the heart, as fire that warms the veins;
> He passed and left my limbs dissolved in dew,
> Relaxed and faint, with passion quivered through;
> Exhausted with spent thrills of dread delight,
> A sudden darkness rushing on my sight.

Eros is like Cupid, drawing back his bow and aiming his arrow at poor girls' hearts. Elsewhere Sappho expressed the feelings of the lovelorn everywhere and through eternity when she wrote, 'Honestly, I wish I were dead.' One story says that she was in love with a man called Phaon, and this love was unrequited. Ovid has her referring to her situation simply as 'my grief'.

The puritanical Stoics didn't seem to have much time for this sort of *eros*. It was at best a distraction from the virtuous life, a passion that should be resisted. While they were not all exactly chaste, they preached that lust was a vice and that in general sex was for procreation. We should guard against *eros* and concentrate on higher things, they reckoned.

Well. If Sappho had been schooled in Stoic principles, and had avoided falling in love, she might have led a happier life. But she wouldn't have become one of the greatest lyric poets the world has ever produced. Fire warming the veins, limbs dissolved in dew and soul-shaking winds are wonderful, stirring images. Similarly, one wonders whether, if Keats's parents had sent him to a Stoic teacher, the world would have been deprived of 'An Ode to Melancholy'. A world comprised solely of Stoic sages who have successfully resisted the passions might be a little boring. No tragedy, no pop music, no Leonard Cohen, no Joy Division. Are the Stoics the enemy of art? We'll return to this objection later.

Still, in many ways they are obviously right. *Eros* is hell. And how on earth are we to defend ourselves, the Stoics will ask, against this powerful disruptor and unnerver of limbs, that can make everyone from old men to young girls go completely mad? How can we retain *apatheia* or indifference to this savage sower of disorder?

As we've seen already, the Stoics were massive fans of Socrates. They praise his heroic and hyper-virtuous continence in the face of multiple attempts by Alcibiades, Athens' sexiest son, to seduce him. This was a man so attractive that togas fell to the ground of their own accord when he appeared. He had an affair with the wife of the Spartan leader. He was famously lustful, and used to visit high-class brothels. Sometimes Socrates, once again seen as chaste and continent, would hunt for him at night in these hotbeds of sin. Alcibiades should have his mind on higher things.

So to be 'Stoic' in matters of love became shorthand for heroically resisting sexual advances, as Socrates had done with Alcibiades. Many centuries later, Lord Byron had a fling in Italy with 18-year-old Claire Clairmont, stepdaughter of Romantic godfather William Godwin and stepsister of Mary Shelley. Mary and Percy Shelley had run away together, and Claire had joined them. The three of them trekked across Europe to find Byron's house in Geneva. Here Claire practically threw herself at the world's sexiest poet, the Alcibiades of his age. 'What could I do?' Lord Byron later said.

> A foolish girl – in spite of all I could say or do –
> would come after me – or rather went before me – for
> I found her here . . . I could not exactly play the Stoic
> with a woman – who had scrambled eight hundred
> miles to unphilosophize me.

Here Byron uses the term 'Stoic' to mean something like 'celibate' or 'chaste', and 'unphilosophize' to mean 'to hell with your lofty musings on the divine, let's have sex right now!' Byron claims, disingenuously, that he was powerless to resist her advances.

Other Stoics urged restraint. Zeno, the original Stoic, survives through the account of his life told by Diogenes Laertius. Early on we get the impression that Zeno preached temperance and the life of the mind. King Antigonus had written to him to ask him to pay him a visit and teach him some philosophy. But Zeno, who was 80 at the time, writes back to say that he cannot accept the invitation, due to 'bodily weakness'. He talks in this letter of the wisdom of embracing philosophy and turning away 'from the much-vaunted pleasure which renders effeminate the souls of some of the young'.

Diogenes Laertius says Zeno was well-known for his 'virtue and temperance', and again we find the ancient philosophers coming across as proto-monks. We're told Zeno died at 98, as proof that he lived a healthy life. He wrote a book called *The Art of Love* but this, sadly, does not survive.

Diogenes says that Zeno and the Stoics count incontinence as a vice. *Apatheia*, or freedom from passion, is a virtue that the Stoic should aim for. The slings and darts of *eros*, in other words, should bounce off the Stoic's armour.

Zeno and the original Stoics, Diogenes goes on, define love as a step on the path towards Platonic companionship. 'Their definition of love is an effort towards friendliness due to visible beauty appearing, its sole end being friendship, not bodily enjoyment . . . love depends on regard.'

However, when it comes to children, the old Greek Stoics seemed to believe in wife-swapping, according to Diogenes Laertius.

> It is also their doctrine that among the wise there should be a community of wives with free choice of partners . . . under such circumstances we shall feel paternal affection for all the children alike, and there will be an end to the jealousies arising from adultery.

A similar idea was proposed in Plato's *Republic* by Socrates. The top people should rise above petty lusts and romantic attachment and devote themselves to virtue, or *arete* in the Greek. Their couplings should be for the purpose of producing children, and should be anonymous. He proposed regular orgies in the countryside for the elite. Maybe this still happens today in the Cotswolds; I wouldn't know. Certainly it was the belief of both Shelley's circle and the Bloomsbury Group that jealousy was a bourgeois contrivance, and that the truly ennobled and enlightened should rise above it (with disastrous results, haha).

Seneca, the Roman Stoic, statesman and rich man, tutor of Nero, reckons that we should all avoid *eros* at all costs because it's one of the passions. ('Lust', of course, would be labelled a sin by the early Christians, who had very pronounced Stoic tendencies.) The duty of the Stoic is to remain impervious to the passions, and to remain in control. In one of his brilliant letters to Lucian, Seneca quotes another philosopher, Panetius, who was asked whether wise men should fall in love.

> As regards the wise man [*sophos*] we shall see; but as for you and me, who are so lacking in wisdom,

we had better refrain so as to avoid a condition that
is frantic, out of control, enslaved to another, and
lacking in self-worth.

Where love is concerned, he goes on to say, you just can't win. 'If our advances are accepted, we are excited by the other person's favour; if not, we are set on fire by disdain.' He concludes, 'We do better to stay calm.' Seneca was writing at a time when it was common for Romans to pursue their frenzied lusts for girls, boys, women, men and everything in between with wild abandon.

For Epictetus, *eros* would lead to the very common sin of adultery, and adultery was utterly destructive and wrong. In fact, when the subject arises during one of his TED talks to the young men, he gets quite angry. In committing adultery, he asks, what are we doing? In the *Discourses* we read: 'Aren't we destroying good feeling between neighbours, aren't we undermining friendship and the state?'

He then addresses a fictional adulterer.

Since you can't hold the position of friend, can you
hold that of a slave? And who will trust you? Aren't
you willing, then, to be thrown out in your turn onto
a dung heap somewhere, like a useless pot, like a piece
of shit?

We might reflect that the Stoical Christ said something similar, though in politer terms. In the audience, one of Epictetus's students says that he thought he'd been taught that women should be considered to be common property, in order to avoid jealousy, which is what we might call the Greek or Bloomsburian or Platonic view of *eros*.

Epictetus turns on the student and compares him to a greedy guest at a dinner party.

> Yes, and a little pig is the common property of those who have been invited to a meal. But when the portions have been handed out, go and grab the share of the person sitting next to you, steal it surreptitiously, or reach out your hand to satisfy your greed.

Piling on the sarcasm, he adds, 'A fine table companion you'd make, a dinner guest worthy of Socrates!'

What does Socrates say about love in Plato's *Symposium*? Here Socrates says that he learned about love from Diotima, a high priestess. She tells Socrates that love is not in fact a god. Rather, he 'is neither mortal or immortal, but something in between'. He is a 'great daimon'.

It's Socrates' speech on love in the *Symposium* – written of course by Plato – that leads to the concept of Platonic love. Socrates sees love as a ladder. It starts with carnal love and then grows into a loving partnership between two people. Finally it ends as pure, divine, monk-like contemplation. Hence the proto-Christian notion that human beings should rise above lust and devote their lives to God. Think of the Stoical St Augustine, a non-stop shagger in early life who later became an actual saint.

Socrates himself presents a confusing example. On the one hand, he shows admirable self-control and even *apatheia* as he resists the multiple advances of Alcibiades. On the other hand, he did gaze admiringly at lots of men, just as Sappho gazed admiringly at lots of women. Both Sappho and Socrates, says the minor poet Maximus of Tyre, 'loved many, and were captivated by things beautiful'. So as good Stoics we should contemplate the beautiful, but without trying to shag it.

Socrates, who had three children with the shrewish Xanthippe, famously loved the beautiful young man Phaedrus. As you probably know, pederastical love, i.e. the love between an older man and a teenage boy, was commonplace in ancient Athens, though was not approved by the state. The 18-year-old Marcus Aurelius, who later in life became Roman emperor and was an important Stoic, fell madly in love with his tutor, Fronto, who was 39. 'Socrates didn't burn more with desire for Phaedrus than I've burned during these days,' he declared to him – 'did I say days? I mean months – for the sight of you.'

In one dialogue Socrates advises that if you encounter a very sexy young man or woman, and find yourself starting to fancy that person, you should run away from them as fast as possible. He advises men to visit prostitutes rather than commit adultery. Brothels were a feature of ancient Athens. He wasn't the only moralist of ancient times to praise the brothel. The stern statesman Cato approved of buying sex, according to Horace in one of his *Satires* (1.2.31–6):

> 'A blessing be with your manliness', he apparently said
> to a young man who was returning from a brothel.
> 'For when loathsome lust has similarly swelled the
> veins, it's right that young men come down here,
> rather than grind through other men's wives.'

Paying for sex with a prostitute, then, is seen as a lesser evil than committing adultery, because affairs can destroy families. Much later St Augustine came to a similar conclusion. 'Let there be an abundance of public prostitutes, whether for anyone who would have the pleasure, or chiefly for those who are not able to have one and are deprived,' he suggests in *City of God*. Note to adulterers: better for the world to call up an escort agency when assailed by *eros*.

I wonder what the ancient women thought about this. It would be good to hear their voices. Certainly we know that the Cynic philosopher Hipparchia was pretty bohemian. She insisted on accompanying her husband Crates to dinner parties, which were customarily all-male occasions (apart from entertainment in the form of flute and dancing girls). She reportedly made love to Crates in public, though we don't know whether they had other partners.

Very curiously, Seneca the Stoic thinks that it's morally wrong to lust after your own wife. His definition of love or *eros* is 'a friendship gone mad'. However, he is also fiercely opposed to adultery. So how, we ask, should the husband manage his lust? After all, he knows that adultery is wrong. For Seneca, it's a case of simply repeating the anti-adultery message to yourself again and again. In Letter to Lucilius number 94 he writes,

> You know that a man who demands chastity from his wife, while seducing other men's wives, is a villain. You know that, just as she should have no dealings with an adulterer, you should have none with a mistress, but you don't act accordingly. Hence you need to have your attention called to these points over and over. These principles should not be stored away but readily at hand.

Epictetus has a similar attitude towards the passion of *eros*. He sees resisting it as a conscious act and something you get better at with practice. You should feel real joy when you successfully train yourself to stop wanting to sleep with every pretty girl or boy you see. 'Don't feed the habit,' he advises, and imagines a small victory in the life of an aspiring Stoic.

> Today, when I saw an attractive boy or woman, I didn't
> say to myself, 'If only I could sleep with her' . . .
> I didn't even go on to picture what happens next, the
> woman being with me, and undressing, and lying
> down beside me.

Epictetus goes on to cite the example of Socrates and his resistance to the advances of the electrifying sex god Alcibiades.

> Go to Socrates and watch him as he lies down beside
> Alcibiades and makes fun of his youthful beauty;
> consider what a victory it was that he won . . . a
> victory worthy of Olympia.

This is not a million miles away from the frequent injunctions in Christian writings to resist looking at your neighbour's wife with adulterous eyes. It also shows us that adultery is as old as the hills and has always been a problem. But the Stoic philosophers address the problem in a slightly different way. Where the Christians ban adultery simply for moral reasons, the Stoics argue that resisting the passion of lust is good for your soul, and can be a source of satisfaction in itself. We should remain impassive and indifferent – just as Byron should have done when Claire Clairmont threw herself at him. Marcus Aurelius says that the Stoic will be able to look with 'chaste eyes' on 'the attractive loveliness of young persons'. He goes on: 'Adorn thyself with simplicity and modesty and with indifference towards the things which lie between virtue and vice. Love mankind. Follow God.'

This all seems very counter-intuitive to the sex-mad, porn-addicted culture of the modern West, where the conventional wisdom seems to be that you should follow your lusts and have as much sex as possible. The Stoics' advice is to cultivate the nobler pleasure that comes from self-mastery, and ascend to a higher plane of love. We can turn the energy of *eros* into something creative rather than destructive. Lust can be transformed into love for the world and for God.

In the ancient world, men were criticized for sleeping with their slaves. In more recent history, for sleeping with the parlour maids. Today it's female interns in offices who are likely to be on the receiving end of libidinous bosses. Just stop it, say the Stoics. Grow up and man up.

The Stoics preached a kind of brotherly love for the whole world. This is connected to their idea of being a *kosmopolites*, a citizen of the universe, a word they'd picked up from Diogenes the Cynic, grandfather of the Stoics, who seems to have coined it, of which more later.

The message to love everyone equally and to consider oneself a citizen of the cosmos should surely be heeded today. When it comes to love, we're encouraged to be thoroughly selfish and to please ourselves by going on a dating app to find the perfect match, some sort of fantasy partner. We've seen countless examples of celebrities who, once they have found the fame and money that they dreamed of, treat people like shit. This is not the Stoic way. For them love, *eros*, was a force that should be channelled towards the good of mankind, not merely indulged in carnal fashion.

And when it comes to citizenship, what used to be called jingoism is all the rage again today. Jingoism meant a kind of excessive patriotism and xenophobia. It is the precise opposite of cosmopolitanism. It is the attitude which says, 'I'm going to look after number one and I don't care what happens to my neighbours and enemies.' Tyrants are back, and we should be destroying them with love, not submitting to them and trying to be like them.

The Stoic message to exert self-control and self-mastery in matters of love and sex has clear echoes in the writings of the early Christians. It was people like the reclusive early monk St John Cassian who invented the whole notion of the seven deadly sins (they're not mentioned in the Bible). They have a lot in common with Stoic principles. They're what Rowan Williams has called the 'passions of the soul'. In the next chapter, on anger, we'll remind ourselves of what they were.

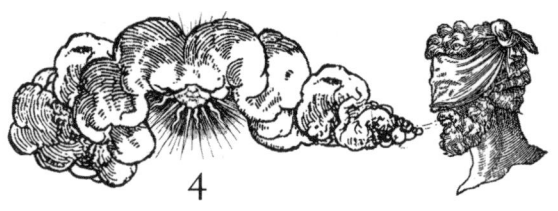

4

Anger

Seneca said that whenever you feel the onset of anger, the best way to contain it is simply to be quite still and to do nothing.

TOLSTOY

We've heard how the Stoics had a sort of proto-Christian attitude when it came to love and sex. However fun and exciting it might be, *eros*, they argued, meaning lust or passionate love, was a destructive demon and should be resisted. Epictetus cited the example of Socrates and his impressive resistance to the advances of the gorgeous Alcibiades. We should all show the same sort of restraint, he said, and feel proud not to give in to our lusts.

But what about Stoic ethics when it came to anger and other passions?

Let's look at the origins of the seven deadly sins in the fourth century AD. We'll be returning to these naughty devils through this book. They're passions to be resisted, and look very much as though they were influenced by the Stoics, though academics can find no solid evidence of a link. The first point to make is that there were originally eight of them. They were invented by the zealous monks of the early Christian period. The monks were attempting to live a pure and chaste life, living on roots and berries, wandering around the desert. But they were assailed by various demons in the form of passions and sins. These demons attempted to divert the poor monks from the path of righteousness. There's a famous painting of the temptation of St Anthony that gives a flavour of what I'm talking about.

The writings of these early Christians are collected into an anthology called *The Philokalia*, meaning 'love of beauty' (compare *philosophia*, meaning love of wisdom). The book was published by Faber and Faber under the orders of T. S. Eliot. One of these crazy hermits, St John of Evagrius, came up with eight vices. Bear them in mind as we explore Stoic thought in this book; all of them are mentioned in one form or another by the Stoics.

First vice: Gluttony
Second vice: Fornication
Third vice: Love of money
Fourth vice: Anger
Fifth vice: Sadness
Sixth vice: Sloth or *acedia*
Seventh vice: Vainglory or self-esteem
Eight vice: Pride

These passions were soon reduced to seven, probably because it's an easier number to remember: seven dwarves, seven wonders, the seven ages of man. The Pythagoreans loved the number seven since it corresponded to the seven musical notes. The famous example is the temptation of St Anthony in the desert, a subject favoured by artists from the tenth century to the present day.

Evagrius was clearly intensely Stoicesque, and I suspect that the early (and later) monks stole their look as well as their ideas from the Greek philosophers. It was Socrates and his followers who started the trend for growing a long beard, wandering round barefoot with a threadbare cloak and a stick, rebuking the rich people and living on crusts of bread and handouts. It's a look that has survived to this day. What should we call it? #monkstyle, perhaps.

Some years ago I asked the great theologian Rowan Williams whether he thought the early Christians were influenced by the Stoics. He replied that he did not doubt it. 'You have Christians trying to establish their credentials in the intellectual world. They say, "Some of this might sound new, but you've heard it before, whether it's Socrates, or Stoics, or Cynics."'

The whole basis of Stoicism is the mastery of the passions. Epictetus, in his *Discourses*, keeps repeating the basic Stoic tenet: stop trying to control the things you can't control, and start controlling the things you can control. Some things are in our power, and some are not. It's up to us. We should use our rationality to stop ourselves being flipped around by our emotions like a ball in a pinball machine. We should cultivate *apatheia*, which to the Stoics did not mean 'apathy' in the sense of sneering indifference. It meant remaining calm, detached, and yes, emotionless. *A* = without and *pathos* = emotion.

Things we can't control might include war, disease and the actions of others. How much energy we waste, say the Stoics, in attempting to force outcomes, rather than letting things happen! Yes, there are shades of Zen Buddhism in the Stoics: go with the flow. And funnily enough Zen Buddhism sprang up at a similar time, in the fifth century BC.

Then there are the things we *can* control. We can control our reactions to events. Even in prison or in chains or in exile, we can remain calm, says Epictetus: 'You can chain my leg, but not even Zeus can overcome my power of choice.'

Epictetus is probably referring to the chains that Socrates wore on his legs while waiting in prison for his execution. Epictetus reckons we should rise above the physical body and its complaints. He refers to 'my poor body', and even illness, he says, should not affect our well-being. The death of a child, the agony of being tortured, the humiliation of being exiled, even the death sentence – none of these common travails of the ancient world should affect our serenity. Yes, it's a pretty tall order. We may never get there. But we can make a start.

For Epictetus we humans are semi-godlike, and need to distinguish ourselves from the animals: 'We're all first and foremost children of God.' Here we note, by the way, Epictetus's monotheism, another Christian element of Stoic thinking. God or Zeus – the terms are used interchangeably – has given us rationality and free will. That means we are all capable of resisting the passions or sins and behaving virtuously. It may not be easy. But it is theoretically possible, and those of us who profess to believe in philosophy should make every effort to become godlike in our reactions. We should become virtuous; that way lies happiness.

Let's take anger. Seneca is against it. In Letter 18 to Lucilius he warns:

> It is like fire: what matters is not the size of the flame but what is in its path. Where the material is solid, even the biggest blaze does not ignite it; dry and

combustible stuff, though, catches even a spark and makes of it an inferno. That's how it is, dear Lucilius: the outcome of anger is madness. Hence we should avoid anger.

Marcus Aurelius, similarly, sees anger as bad. At the beginning of his *Meditations* he praises his friend Sextus for his level-headedness. '[He] never showed anger or any other passion, but was entirely free from passion, and also most affectionate.' Marcus rebukes those who argue that there is something macho about losing your temper.

> And let this truth be present to thee in the excitement of anger, that to be moved by passion is not manly, but that mildness and gentleness, as they are more agreeable to human nature, so also are they more manly.

The Stoics talk about 'submitting' to anger. The free and happy person, they say, would not obey such a despotic master. Submitting to anger lowers you to the level of a slave. Epictetus says you should refrain from being angry even from those who do you wrong. Your anger is not actually the fault of the thief or the adulterer. In the *Discourses* he says that it's your fault for getting attached to objects or other human beings.

> Why, then, are we angry? Because we attach value to things that these people steal from us. Well, stop attaching such value to our clothes, and you won't be angry with the man who steals them. Don't attach value to the beauty of your wife and you won't be angry with the thief and the adulterer.

The truly enlightened Stoic doesn't care if his wife is unfaithful or his house gets burgled. 'Recognize that a thief and an adulterer belong not among the things you own, but only among those that are someone else's and aren't within your power.'

We might think: *wow*. Imagine being so serene that you can react with equanimity if your partner cheats on you or your friend steals all your money. That would be good, I suppose. It would make you invincible. 'Who, then, is the invincible human being?' he asks in the *Discourses*. 'One who can be disconcerted by nothing that lies outside the sphere of choice.' Epictetus tells a little anecdote to illustrate his point. He says he was sleeping one night when he heard a noise. He went downstairs to discover that an iron lamp of his, which stood in front of his household gods, had been stolen. 'What of it?' he says to himself. 'Tomorrow you'll find yourself an earthenware lamp.'

During another lesson he's asked by a student how to stop his brother being angry with him. Epictetus tells him that he can't, and shouldn't bother. He should instead concentrate on his own reactions. I don't need to tell you, I guess, that this insistence on choosing your reactions to external events, which lie outside of your control, is a key tenet of cognitive behavioural therapy and countless modern self-help books. Most of these Stoic-influenced books and therapies sidestep the deep religious component of the Stoics – their belief in providence and God and so on – but we'll come back to that.

In attempting to describe Stoic doctrine in his essay on Zeno, Diogenes Laertius mentions the vices. The principal ones, he says, are 'folly and cowardice and injustice and intemperance'. Temperance can be seen as a resistance to the snares of passions like anger. Above all the

Stoic sage must remain impassive, impervious, serene and calm. He is searching for *ataraxia*, or 'tranquillity', 'undisturbedness' (*a* = without and *traxia* = confusion). Socrates never lost his temper when arguing and philosophizing, notes Epictetus.

Epictetus says we should remain grateful for the wonderful world that God has created. Surely it's no accident, he says, that we have these fantastic brains. Sex, too, is incredible: 'And male and female, and the desire that they have for intercourse with one another, and the power they have to make use of the organs that have been constructed for that purpose, do these things not reveal their maker either?

The philosopher gets so excited by the world that he goes on to write a short hymn of praise to the creator, refuting the atheists of the time.

> Great is God, for having provided us with these
> implements with which we till the earth; great is God
> for having given us hands, and the power to swallow,
> and a stomach, and enabling us to grow without
> thinking of it, and to breathe while we're asleep . . . I am
> a rational being, and I must sing the praise of God.

Again, this sounds very Christian.

It's from the Stoics that we get the phrase 'go with the flow', more commonly associated with hippies and a vague Orientalism. The everyday slings and arrows of life will not disturb us if we realize there is a grander plan at work. Like a Taoist we should not waste a lot of energy trying to control the external world. Leave it alone and concentrate on your own virtue. Be as tranquil as a god. 'It is amazing what power there is in philosophy to beat back all the assaults of chance', writes the Roman Stoic (and contemporary of Christ) Seneca in his Letter number 54 to Lucilius.

> No weapon lodges in its flesh; its defences cannot be penetrated. When fortune's darts come in, it either ducks and lets them pass by, or stands its ground and lets them bounce back against the assailant.

Seneca, though, doesn't have much time for virtue signalling. He reckons that the Stoic should live a fairly normal life. As soon as you go weird and throw your clothes away and live in a hole in the ground and grow a smelly beard and stop washing, you alienate others from the Stoic creed. You make philosophy look silly and difficult. And, he says, you draw attention to yourself. The same criticism was levelled at the Greek Cynics: their radical and obvious pink-like rejection of worldly vanity was itself a form of vanity.

This brings to mind Dickens' story about the mad hermit. In his 1861 book *The Uncommercial Traveller* he writes about meeting a crazy recluse called Mr Mopes. This character was based on a real-life character of the day called 'Mad Lucas'. Lucas was the heir to a fortune but chose to live in a dungeon, dress in rags and sleep in soot and cinders with the rats. This modern-day anchorite became a bit of a celebrity: postcards were produced of him. But Dickens had no time for the vanity of this modern-day Cynic. 'I know you like to be seen,' he says to him when he visits. 'Vanity, all is vanity.'

Again in proto-Christian fashion, the Stoics were fiercely opposed to gluttony. It was a Roman vice. The Stoic texts teem with references to Romans and Greeks vomiting in the street following an excess of wine.

Not so the Stoics. 'They drink wine', says Diogenes Laertius of the Stoics, 'but they do not get drunk; and they never yield to frenzy.' In the *Symposium* Socrates had famously drunk everyone under the table, but did not get even mildly tipsy. In a letter Seneca says that during Saturnalia, December's festival of self-indulgence, the bold Stoic should 'remain cold sober when everyone else is drunk and vomiting'. Either that or drink moderately. And he was not a fan of the Roman party town of Baiae near Naples, the Ibiza of its day, where he stayed for a few days. He complains about 'the adulterous ladies sailing by, the many kinds of pleasure boats painted in different colours, the roses floating all over the lagoon . . . the musicians' nightly racket'.

Hmm. Baiae doesn't sound that bad to me. And Seneca's alternative to Baiae is very unattractive indeed. A real man, he says, a Stoic sage, would, instead of going on a hedonistic holiday, wander round with a spade and dig a hole to sleep in. He should 'remain within some trench works dug with his own hand for a single night's use'. Nice.

Seneca's professed asceticism is perhaps a little galling because we know that he was fabulously wealthy and owned several villas and many slaves, having been top courtier to Nero and also a moneylender.

Well. The idea that you should become entirely free of emotion is perhaps an odd notion to us today. We're more inclined to think that it's a good idea to let it all out. The emotionless man would be something like the Mekon, or a Dalek, perhaps.

And anyway, the early Christians, Stoic as they were, had what Rowan Williams has called a 'soft spot for anger'. In *Passions of the Soul*, which is all about the seven deadly sins, he says that anger can be a positive force, and cites one of the early monks, John Cassian.

> The proper use, the proper understanding of anger, according to Cassian and others, is that it is something that has to be focused on our own malicious and destructive thoughts, and on the destructiveness around us. It has a proper use, and in this literature it is often the cardinal example of how the 'passions of the soul' are natural instincts that should not be simply denied or repressed, but which do, emphatically and urgently, need to be named and understood in terms of their proper purpose.

That more tolerant Christian attitude to anger takes off the rough edge off extreme Stoicism: we should not feel bad when we experience the passion of anger. It's natural. The thing is what you then do with it. It could be a destructive or a creative force. 'Anger is an energy,' said John Lydon, and think of all the great art, books, social movements and music that have been inspired by righteous fury. We might mention the abolition of child labour and slavery, for example. The Suffragettes were very angry indeed.

It's also worth mentioning here that to be a Stoic sage is an aspiration that can never be fulfilled. Only Socrates and possibly Diogenes of Sinope ever came close. To be perfectly Stoic is an impossible aspiration. It's the same with being a tennis player. I play tennis and I hope to improve as the years go by. Obviously I will never play as well as Roger Federer. But I can still call myself a tennis player. In the same way, I can call myself a Stoic without claiming to be perfectly dispassionate and ataractic when someone throws a stone at me. And as with tennis, I recognize that if I want to be a Stoic, I need to train regularly.

Of course, we can think of some practical ways of avoiding the seductions of anger and greed and the other demons. Avoiding social media is one simple strategy. Social media sells advertising by stimulating the passions. It has monetized the seven deadly sins. Social media loves anger. It makes you angry. It stimulates outrage. It wants you to be angry, and so it delivers you a stream of rage-inducing news, because anger leads to clicks and clicks lead to revenue. Instagram wants you to be envious, jealous, greedy and covetous because that will make you a better consumer. Other passions like lust and pride are clearly encouraged, promoted and monetized by the internet.

Once the algorithm and social media posts have done their work on making you feel useless, insecure, somewhat lacking, envious, anxious or lustful, they will then deliver an advert which promises to solve the problem: make-up, a money-making scheme, a dating app. The bad news, the problem, which is terrible things happening in the world and other people leading a better life than you, is followed by the good news, which is adverts. To allay your misery, buy something. And in California Mark Zuckerberg counts his billions. Developing your Stoic power will help you resist the seductions of these demons.

Maybe it would be a good idea to keep our children away from these passion-raising devices, to raise them to be tough and self-sufficient. This would be the aim of a Stoic education.

Education

> *The greatest and most important difficulty of human sciences is the education of children.*
> MONTAIGNE

When Mary Shelley was 14 years old, her father, the anarchist philosopher William Godwin, sent her to the wilds of Dundee to stay for a few months with a family friend, linen merchant William Baxter. Having dropped off Mary at the dock in Margate for the five-day boat trip, Godwin wrote a letter to Baxter.

> I am anxious that she should be brought up like a philosopher, even like a Cynic. It will add greatly to the strength & worth of her character. I should also observe that she has no love of dissipation, & will be perfectly satisfied with your woods & your mountains.

By 'Cynic' Godwin did not mean that he wanted his daughter to be aloof, amoral, sneery. He meant that he wanted her to acquire a philosophical or Stoical temperament, a disregard for the things people normally value. That would mean a certain monkish disdain for worldly things, a self-reliance and a love of nature, hence the 'woods and mountains'.

Mary's mother, the feminist pioneer Mary Wollstonecraft, had tragically died 11 days after giving birth to her. But thanks in part to Godwin's intellectual approach to fathering, Mary went on to become one of the best writers of her generation. She did, after all, write *Frankenstein*, a work of genius that has gone on to be far better known to the wider world than anything by Shelley or Byron. And she was certainly tough, principled and single-minded: when young she (and Shelley) refused to eat sugar as a protest against the slave trade.

That great wit and essayist Michel de Montaigne had a philosophical father, too. When Montaigne was a baby he was sent to live with the local peasants in the Bordeaux area to toughen him up. Montaigne later wrote approvingly of this scheme and advised others to allow their children to be 'formed by fortune under the laws of the common people and nature'.

Then, very eccentrically, his dad decided that Latin should be his first language, and hired a German Latin teacher called Dr Horst to come and live with the family. Accordingly, Montaigne started speaking Latin when he was two years old. So it was, he said, that he learned Latin 'without a book, without grammar or precept, without the whip and without tears'. Dad also had little Michel woken in the morning with the gentle sounds of the lute rather than a harsh bell, a kind of ambient alarm clock. Montaigne's biographer Sarah Bakewell says that as a result of this philosophical education he, like Mary Shelley, 'grew up to be an independent-minded adult, following his own path in everything rather than deferring to duty and discipline'.

Montaigne later 'identified' as a Stoic, though he certainly had both Epicurean and Sceptic tendencies. In his own essays on education he asks why philosophy is not taught at a much younger age.

> Since philosophy is that which instructs us to live, and that infancy has there its lessons as well as other ages, why is it not communicated to children betimes? . . . take the plain philosophical discourses, learn how rightly to choose, and then rightly apply them; they are more easy to be understood than one of Boccaccio's novels.

The point is that Boccaccio's bawdy tales in the *Decameron* are famously fun and straightforward. I agree here with Montaigne. Anecdotes of the Cynics and of Socrates are not difficult. And they're fun. We should teach ancient philosophy to young children.

Montaigne goes on to recommend a progressive and peaceful approach to teaching.

> Education ought to be carried on with a severe sweetness, quite contrary to the practices of our pedants, who, instead of tempting and alluring children to letters by apt and gentle ways, do in truth present nothing before them but rods and ferrules, horror and cruelty. Away with this violence! Away with this compulsion!

This is of course the precise opposite of the 'stiff upper lip' education meted out to boys at places like Eton in the nineteenth and twentieth centuries, which most of us might think of as 'Stoic'. I remember attending the funeral of an earl. A friend giving a eulogy praised his

'Stoicism', which was something that he'd apparently picked up at Eton in the 1950s. This sort of Flashman version of a Stoic education – holding back the tears while being flogged – is not what Socrates and Epictetus had in mind at all. They believed in dialogue and debate.

Or St Augustine in his *Confessions*, 397 AD. This is a great read – especially the bits about his sex addiction and courtesan habit. Augustine, whose main career was a teacher of rhetoric, complained about being beaten as a boy. He compared the way he was taught Greek – through violence – with the way he learned Latin, which was positively Montaignian.

> Why did I hate the Greek classics? For not one word of it did I understand, and to make me understand I was urged vehemently with cruel threats and punishments. Time was also (as an infant) I knew no Latin; but this I learned without fear or suffering, by mere observation, amid the caresses of my nursery and jests of friends, smiling and sportively encouraging me. This I learned without any pressure of punishment to urge me on, for my heart urged me to give birth to its conceptions, which I could only do my learning words not of those who taught, but of those who talked with me; in whose ears also I gave birth to the thoughts, whatever I conceived.

Augustine comes down firmly on the side of the educational progressives.

'No doubt, then, that a free curiosity has more force in our learning these things, than a frightful enforcement.'

All this is not to say that the Stoic child should be wrapped in cotton wool and protected from all pain.

Socrates was known for being physically tough – he walked barefoot on ice, after all – and Stoics from Epictetus to Seneca agree that it's wise to accustom yourself – and your children – to hardship.

John Locke was inspired by the Stoics in his childcare manual, *Some Thoughts Concerning Education*, published in 1690. He recommended cold baths, citing Seneca who apparently 'used to bathe himself in cold spring water in the midst of winter'. He advocated playing outdoors and also endorsed a vegetarian diet, at least until the child is three or four. 'Most children's constitutions are either spoiled', Locke wrote, 'or at least harmed, by cockering and tenderness.' That lovely seventeenth-century word 'cockering' means 'to indulge or spoil'. He went on to recommend that children are not too warmly wrapped up in winter, in order that they learn to endure cold, like the Spartans. He also reckons that the shoes of children should be made deliberately leaky in order to toughen up the feet.

In Letter 33 Seneca has some tips for teachers of children.

> Individual sayings take hold more easily when they are isolated and rounded off like bits of verse. That is why we give children proverbs to memorize, and what the Greeks call *chreiai*: they are what a child's mind is able to encompass, not yet having room for anything larger.

For Epictetus a Stoic education would continually drive home the notion (later repeated by John Lennon in 'All You Need Is Love') that we're all where we're meant to be.

> Education is precisely learning to will all individual things just as they happen . . . we should proceed to

education not in order to change the conditions (for this is not granted to us nor would it be better) but in order that, with things about us as they are and as their nature is, we may keep our minds in harmony with what happens.

The Roman elite did at least reckon that a philosophical education was an important requirement: Epictetus's students are young men, of course. Not that all Stoics believed women should be excluded. Musonius Rufus, Epictetus's teacher, was a stern advocate – like Plato and Socrates – of the education of women. One of his essays has the leading title, 'Should Daughters Receive the Same Education as Sons?' Women, like men, he says, have the capacity to display all the virtues: reason, justice, temperance and courage. Everyone should be philosophical, he goes on, and philosophy needs to be taught, therefore girls should be taught how to be philosophers:

> [T]hings which have reference to virtue ought to be taught to male and female alike; and furthermore . . . straight from infancy they ought to be taught that this is right and this is wrong, and that it is the same for both alike.

Musonius is no feminist: he wants women to be educated not so that they can have a career, but so they can be better housekeepers. He says a wife should be a 'sympathetic helpmate' to her husband, and be 'chaste and self-controlled'. He concludes by asserting that 'the teachings of philosophy exhort the woman to be content with her lot and to work with her own hands.' Not a particularly inspiring message.

EDUCATION

In the introduction to his *Meditations*, where he praises various teachers he's had, Marcus Aurelius appears to approve of home education. He writes that he learned from his grandfather's father 'to dispense with attendance at public schools, and to enjoy good teachers at home, and to recognize that on such things money should be eagerly spent'. He's also grateful that he was asked to 'write dialogues as a boy'. He also praises one teacher who taught him 'not to keep quails'. I'm not sure why quail-keeping was considered anti-philosophical, but thankfully I can honestly report that not one of my three children has ever kept quails. From his father he says he learned to 'suppress all passion for boys' (this suggests of course that at one stage he did).

Marcus has a nice summary of what the philosopher should not do. It's about ethics, he says, not logical disputation or showing off or speculating about the movements of the planets. He is grateful that 'when I set my heart on philosophy, I did not fall into the hands of a sophist, nor sat down at the author's desk, or become a solver of syllogisms, nor busied myself with physical phenomena.'

When we talk about a Stoic education we should be clear of course that for Stoics learning is a lifelong process. We have the example of Socrates, who took dancing lessons when he was 70. Montaigne approved: 'There is nothing more notable in Socrates than that he found time, when he was an old man, to learn music and dancing, and thought it time well spent.'

Seneca went back to school in his sixties. 'I am taking philosophy lessons!' he wrote to Lucilius in Letter 76.

> Today is the fifth day I have gone to school to hear the philosopher lecturing from two o'clock onward.

'What, at your age?' Why not? What could be more foolish than failing to learn a thing simply because you haven't learned it earlier?

These examples give us a delightful image of two jolly, child-like Stoic men, mature students, hurling themselves cheerfully into schooling.

Let's close this chapter on education with two further Stoic precepts. The first is that learning is within us. This is a point repeated by Socrates. To learn, we need to take the time to look within. To prove this point, in a dialogue with his friend Meno, he takes an uneducated slave boy and proves that the boy can do a tricky maths puzzle. I did this on holiday with some young children, and it worked. Given a bit of time and a bit of prodding, they were able to work out the problem for themselves.

Let's have a go. Draw a square on a piece of paper. Now tell me, how would you now produce a picture of a square that was precisely twice the area of the original square?

Our second precept is: too much book learning is a dangerous thing. The anti-academic strain in philosophy can be traced back to Diogenes of Sinope, who felt that Plato's classes were a waste of time. Just wander around the woods. Be natural. And like Montaigne after him he believed that the peasants had a better understanding of a philosophical approach to life than the gentry and the elite.

This is what the anecdote of the wooden bowl is all about. Diogenes – a banker's son – is out wandering when he sees a peasant boy drinking water from the stream by cupping his hands. The Cynic philosopher, who, like Socrates, was admired by the frugal Stoics, then looks at one of his few remaining possessions, a wooden bowl.

'What an absurd encumbrance!' he shouts, and flings the bowl into the woods.

Montaigne likewise writes on how the ordinary people who live near him suffer death and illness cheerfully. He goes on to warn against an excess of education, quoting Seneca: 'In learning as in everything else, we suffer from lack of moderation.' 'We hardly need any learning to live at our ease,' Montaigne goes on.

> And Socrates teaches us that this learning lies within us, as well as how to find it there and how to get help from it. All the ability of ours for exceeding what is natural is pretty much vain and superfluous.

He concludes with another morsel of Senecan wisdom: 'Little learning is needed to form a good mind.'

But a little learning should be taught. I'm with Montaigne: philosophy should be on the curriculum from a young age. Schools teach Bible stories. Why not tales from the life of Socrates?

Well. Montaigne had retired from politics to become a full-time philosopher at the age of 35. Socrates pretty much avoided it for most of his life. Seneca and Cicero, on the other hand, were thrust deep into it until old age, when they spent a lot of time philosophizing. And of course Marcus Aurelius was a real-life Roman emperor. So how much should the Stoic engage in political life? That's the subject of our next chapter.

Answer to puzzle: The slave boy, after a couple of false starts, correctly concludes that one side of the new square is produced by drawing a diagonal line connecting the two opposite corners of the original, and creating a new square by drawing the other three sides. Simples!

6

Politics

Happy is the man who has broken the chains which hurt the mind, and has given up worrying once and for all.
OVID, *REMEDIA AMORIS*, 293–4

Polites ei tu kosmou (*you are a citizen of the world*).
EPICTETUS

You have doubtless heard people complain that 'politics has become divisive'. Commentators in the pub or on social media or in the newspapers point to Brexit or Trump and say that politics is now toxic and splits people into two opposing camps. These comments imply that at some point in the past politics was not divisive, but somehow harmonizing.

This is a supremely naive thing to say. Politics is by its nature divisive, and always has been. The voters are generally asked to choose between two candidates. We are therefore instantly divided into mutually loathing camps. And it's always been this way. Guelfs and Ghibellines, Tories and Whigs, Republicans and Democrats, Remainers and Brexiteers – all fighting each other like cats and dogs, completely unable or unwilling to see things from the other person's point of view.

Ancient Greece and Rome were of course no different. From the self-governing city state of Athens to the gigantic Roman Empire, divisions, factions, wars, deaths, assassinations, court cases, plots, intrigues, coups and all the rest were a daily feature. Julius Caesar was quite Trump-like: he entertained the ordinary people, became rich and spent lavishly.

However, politics has another meaning. It's derived from the word *polis* for city. So the word also means something like 'the art of city management'. And as members of self-ruling city states, the Stoics believed that each male adult citizen had a duty to contribute time and thinking to the wider community.

Man, they believed, is naturally political. And he is not only part of his city. He is also a cosmopolitan, a member of the cosmos. In a sense, every act is therefore political.

But what was the best way to benefit your community? To contemplate, or to act?

If we take the example of Socrates, as the Stoic thinkers regularly do in order to prove their arguments, then we find something of a paradox. Socrates was intimate with the politicians of the era. He had taught Alcibiades. He had long conversations with the brilliant Aspasia, girlfriend of Pericles, the de facto ruler of Athens. He was involved with the everyday life of Athens. He wanted what was best for his city. But he did not enter the political game.

In the startlingly unapologetic *Apology*, Plato's account of the speeches he made at his trial, Socrates tells the 500 assembled jurors why he avoids politics. He explains that his inner demon, or conscience, warned him away:

> It is a sort of voice that comes to me, and when
> it comes it always holds me back from what I am

thinking of doing, but never urges me forward. This it is which opposes my engaging in politics. And I think this opposition is a very good thing; for you may be quite sure, men of Athens, that if I had undertaken to go into politics, I should have been put to death long ago and should have done no good to you or to myself.

In other words, if you want to speak the truth, then it's best to do it without getting directly involved with the administration of the state. Perhaps Socrates also found politics to be too compromising. In the UK, for sure, MPs complain that they're not allowed to vote with their own conscience, but have to toe the party line. The inner demon, the divine voice, must be ignored. Socrates is saying that he would have been completely honest and therefore would have been executed! To make an obvious point, then, politics is political. It divides people and it demands compromise and expediency. It almost forces you to lie. This will not bring happiness. After all, the Greek word for happiness, *eudaimonia*, translates literally as 'good demon-ness'. It means being at one with your inner demon – certainly not ignoring it.

Socrates is also arguing that by avoiding political engagement and concentrating on philosophy, he's had a much longer career and a happy death. After all, he lived to 70, was still taking dancing lessons, and died not of old age, but of the hemlock. Compare his fate with that of the lawyer and philosopher Cicero. He'd only been retired from politics for a couple of years when, at just 63, he was murdered by order of his enemy Mark Antony. And as we know, Antony's wife Fulvia spat on Cicero's severed head, then laid it in her lap, took some pins out of her hair and stuck them into Cicero's tongue. You can't say the Romans weren't theatrical.

Having said all this, the Stoics did not believe, like the Epicureans, that the answer to anxiety and stress was to leave the city and settle in a self-sufficient farming commune. And we can't all be Socrates, or indeed Christ. Most of us have to earn a living and engage to some degree in the everyday life of our village or town or city or country.

Our first Stoic, Zeno, was reportedly 98 when he died. He was not a politician but a full-time teacher, instructing the young men of Athens in the ways of temperance and virtue. 'Zeno was the first to designate as the end "life in agreement with nature",' says Diogenes Laertius, 'which is the same as a virtuous life.' As you know, the Stoics reckoned that external goods like money and fame and renown were to be treated with indifference. They're neither bad nor good, but we should not rely on them for our personal happiness as they may get taken away from us with a moment's notice.

You might expect Zeno, therefore, to recommend steering clear of political life, as Socrates had done. But there is a different argument. The Stoic mission to cultivate temperance and virtue in mankind can be helped by sensible politicking. Says Diogenes Laertius:

> The Stoics say that the wise man will take part in politics . . . for thus he will restrain vice and promote virtue . . . the wise man is naturally made for society and action.

Both Zeno and Chrysippus, according to Plutarch, wrote books called *Politeia*, as did Plato (we translate this as *The Republic*), about their ideal society. These both promoted the aspiration of being a *kosmopolites*, a citizen of the world, without need for city walls. Plutarch wrote:

> [T]he much-admired Republic of Zeno, the founder of the Stoic sect, may be summed up in this one main principle: that all the inhabitants of this world of ours should not live differentiated by their respective rules of justice into separate cities and communities, but that we should consider all men to be of one community and one polity.

Zeno, we're told, would ban money, law courts and gymnasia from his republic. He also proposed free love and unisex clothing as a way of promoting harmony. I guess that these *politeias*, like the utopias written by Thomas More and others in later millennia, were really a starting point for discussion, and a comment on the existing state of things, rather than a practical proposal.

It was a sensible idea to discuss how society could be better arranged. Cicero makes a similar point in his Tusculan Disputation on happiness: 'Let the wise man we have discussed also pass to the maintenance of the public weal' (the Latin here is *rem publicam*, literally 'the public thing', but often translated as 'the commonwealth', hence 'republic').

> What course more excellent could he take, since his prudence shows him the true advantage of his fellow citizens, his justice lets nothing of theirs divert to his own family, and he is strong in the exercise of so many different remaining virtues?

Did Boris become Mayor of London for the good of the public weal? Did Trump enter politics for the betterment of the people? No. Tyrants are the opposite of philosophers. They are anti-wisdom. We should call them *katasophers*. (*Kata* means 'against' or 'down', as in *katastrophe*, meaning 'down turn'.)

And of course there were well-known and very active politicians in ancient Rome who we'd call Stoic. We can look to the example of Cato the Younger. Seneca and Cicero frequently mention him as an example of admirable fortitude in the face of opposition (more on his suicide in our chapter on death).

'Get involved', then, seemed to be the standard Stoic advice. Don't run away, like the pleasure-embracing Epicureans, who lived in self-sufficient gardening communes and avoided both pain and politics. Go into the marketplace and be in the world. These arguments persist today. A pal of mine is the economist Guy Standing, best known for his ceaseless advocacy of a Citizen's Income. I'd written a short essay in the *Idler* magazine which recommended that philosophically inclined people should steer clear of politics.

'I profoundly disagree with you', Standing objected,

> in calling for Idlers to abstain from politics. One should differentiate between being a politician and being politically active. As argued in my book on time, the ancient Athenians believed the defining virtue of a citizen was spending as much time as possible in *schole*, which was a combination of public participation in the life of the polis and education. This required adequate *aergia*, idleness, to give time for balanced reflection. The Greeks understood that

the long-term health of democracy required the active participation of the citizenry in political life. They knew that if people ceased to be participatory there would be a drift to tyranny, run by the oligarchy. Such was their conviction that popular involvement was vital that they even had a word for those who did not participate. The word was *idiotai* . . . Absenting oneself from political participation is to risk surrendering your humanity to the incipient tyrants.

Oi, Standing, are you calling me an idiot? We could argue that tyranny has emerged from democracy: the tyrant Trump has conquered despite the political participation of many opponents. And Epictetus says that the pure philosopher should avoid practical matters. His mind is on higher things. Speaking of the ideal Cynic philosopher – someone like Diogenes, who called himself a 'cosmopolitan' – he says:

> If you care to, ask me whether he should get involved in public affairs. Blockhead, can you think of any higher business than that in which he is already engaged? Or would you have him step forward at Athens to speak about revenues and resources when it is his business to speak to all of humanity, Athenian, Corinthian and Roman alike . . . about happiness and unhappiness, about good and bad, about freedom and servitude? Ask me too whether he'll take any public post, and I'll reply again, Fool, what post could be more important than that which he already holds?

Seneca is well aware of the conventional Stoic view that people should engage in public service. He quotes

Zeno: 'The sage will take part in politics unless it is unavoidable.' However, he then argues that retiring from the hurly-burly – in other words, becoming an idler – is itself a form of service. In a letter to Lucilius (no. 68), who has clearly expressed a wish to retire from the busy world, he expands the definition of 'state' to mean 'mankind'.

> I support your plan: hide yourself away in leisure . . . When we [Stoics] enjoin service to the state, we do not mean to just any state, nor that one must serve at all times or without ending. Besides, we assign to the wise man a state worthy of him, that is, the whole world. Thus he is not outside the state even if he does retire.

In his essay *De Otia*, which I would translate as 'On Idling', he expands on this argument.

> Even if we try no other medicine, withdrawal in itself will be beneficial: we will be better when alone. Moreover, then we may withdraw among the best men and choose some example towards which we may turn our lives. This only comes about in leisure.

Note that the Latin word for business is *negotium* or 'not-leisure'. In a sense, then, the Stoics would consider *negotium* to be a waste of time, while *otium* is the proper use of one's time, the reverse of the dominant attitude of the twenty-first century, which is that work is the important thing and leisure only important insofar as it recharges you for more work.

Anyway, Seneca then imagines an interlocutor objecting to his embrace of idling.

What are you saying, Seneca? Are you deserting your party? Surely your Stoics say, 'Right up to the very end of life we shall be in motion, we should not cease working for the common good, helping individuals, giving strength even to our enemies with our elderly hand. We are those who give no years to exemption from military service and, as that most eloquent man said, 'We conceal our grey hair with a helmet' [Virgil, *Aeneid*, 9.612].'

He then argues that, following a life of public service, it's perfectly admissible to retire and embrace philosophy full-time. '[S]omeone has the full right to do this at a far-advanced age, when his service is completed, and pass it on to others while his mind is sharpest.'

I'd add that if you're seeking *ataraxia* in life, then surely politics should be avoided, because politics is a battle, and in most battles there are two losers. To search for glory or public approval will cause you worry and pain. And the politician's life does not always end well. This is an argument Marvell summed up in his lovely Epicurean poem, 'The Garden':

How vainly men themselves amaze
To win the palm, the oak or bayes.

Epictetus advises his students to stay out of fights:

A virtuous and good person neither quarrels with anyone nor, so far as he can, does he allow anyone else to quarrel. In this matter, as in so much else, an example is set for us in the life of Socrates, who not only made a consistent practice of avoiding quarrels for his own part, but also tried to prevent others from quarrelling.

How different from those politicians who proclaim their love of fighting. How different from social media, which profits from quarrelling and division.

Another worry that besets politicians – and which is encouraged by social media – is concern for your reputation. What do people think of me? Can I get more followers on Twitter? Again, Cicero says that as reputation goes – the Greek word was εὐδοξία, *eudoxia* – you should not care a fig: 'Chrysippus and Diogenes denied its whole utility, and used to say that one ought not even to put forth a finger for the sake of it.' Diogenes had said, 'Bad reputation is an empty noise made by madmen.'

The Stoics took this 'don't care' philosophy to the next level when it came to pain. Unlike the Epicureans, who believed that pleasure should be embraced and pain avoided, the Stoics reckoned that physical or emotional pain was an 'indifferent'. It should not be allowed to get in the way of your happiness. In our modern world, which wants to destroy pain, to 'hit pain where it hurts', in the words of the advert, the aim of remaining indifferent to it is quite an extraordinary idea, and one we'll explore next.

7

Pain

> *A baby who is set on standing up and is getting used to supporting himself . . . falls down and with tears keeps getting up again until he has trained himself through pain what to do what nature demands.*
>
> SENECA

The ancient world was a painful place, if Seneca, in his letters to Lucilius, is to be believed. Agonies lurked everywhere. Torture was a common fear, and the Roman authorities seemed to exhibit a lively imagination when it came to physical punishment.

> Imagine here the jail, the cross, the rack, the hook, the stake driven up through the middle of a person and coming out at the mouth, the limbs torn apart by chariots driven in different directions, the garment woven and smeared with inflammable pitch.

But the Stoics proclaimed indifference to pain. They believed that pain – *ponos* – should not get in the way of your progress towards happiness. They're fond of mentioning the bull of Phalaris. This is named for the fifth-century Sicilian tyrant, who had a model of a bull made of bronze. He would incarcerate his enemy inside this bull and light a fire underneath it, thereby gently roasting the unfortunate occupant.

Seneca says, very surprisingly, that the pleasure-loving Epicurus would actively enjoy such a horrific fate. 'Even Epicurus says that the sage, if roasted in the bull of Phalaris, will say: "It is pleasant. It does not matter to me at all."' Pain and joy: they're all the same, says Seneca. 'There is equality between joy on the one hand and stout-hearted endurance of torture.'

Surely this is madness? Seneca imagines his correspondent Lucilius objecting: are you really saying that joy and the unbending endurance of pain are much of a muchness?

Well, Seneca argues, we experience much pain in everyday life: not only the slings and arrows of outrageous fortune, and the pain of illness or torture, but also self-inflicted torments as we strive for riches or fame or glory. Think of the pain that athletes endure, with no guarantee of getting gold at the end. 'Pain is just an emotion,' the England cricket captain Ben Stokes has said. And a virtuous person would hurl themselves into the river to save a drowning child without thinking about it. So in fact, pain is part of life.

The Stoic believes that it's virtue that makes you happy, not lack of pain, and that it is possible to be virtuous in the midst of pain or in the midst of pleasure. Those of us who have perversely enjoyed a hangover may have an inkling of what he is talking about.

Epictetus says that the role of the philosopher is to banish pain, among other undesirables: 'If you heed me you will feel no pain, no anger, no compulsion, no hindrance, but you will pass your lives in tranquillity and in freedom from every kind of disturbance.' Philosophy promises 'a state of mind undisturbed by passion, pain, fear or confusion – in a word, freedom'.

Cicero, he tells us, decided to lead a seminar on the subject at his house in Tusculum. In the second Tusculan Disputation he argues that you can become accustomed to pain. You can learn to live with it.

> The force of habit is great. Hunters pass the night in the snow on the mountains. Indians suffer themselves to be burnt. Boxers battled by the gauntlets do not so much as utter a groan.

Cicero cites approvingly the example of the Spartan youth who are trained to bear pain:

> The laws of Lycurgus educate youth by hardships, hunting and running, hunger and thirst, exposure to heat and cold; moreover at the altar Spartan boys are submitted to such a shower of stripes [a vivid word for lashings with the whip] that from the flesh the blood comes forth in streams.

It was clearly the school of Sparta that the Victorian schoolmasters had in mind. On the subject of learning how to deal with pain, Dr Johnson remarked to Boswell, 'I am sorry that prize-fighting is gone out . . . Prize-fighting made people accustomed not to be alarmed at seeing their own blood or feeling a little pain from a wound.' For Cicero, the fear of pain is the problem. As with death, the proper Stoic would scorn pain.

> For my part, whatever pain is, I do not think it deserves its apparent importance, and I say that men are unduly influenced by a spurious image of it in our fancy, and that all pain is endurable . . . Man's peculiar virtue is fortitude . . . scorn of death and scorn of pain.

You might reflect on these words when undergoing root canal treatment at the dentist, or the agonizing trials of periodontistry, where the gums are peeled back from the teeth for the purposes of deep cleaning. Scorn the pain! It will be over soon, and it's for a good cause. It's virtuous to bear it without crying out.

Famously, Admiral Stockdale used Stoic teachings to help him to endure torture when a POW in Vietnam. And let's not forget that it still happens today, lest we smugly think that torture died out in the Middle Ages. Take a look at the website for the charity Human Rights Watch. There it's explained that torture is banned under international law, but remains commonplace, and current examples are cited, whether Guantanamo Bay or Palestine.

When it comes to pain, the Stoics reckon, you can remain indifferent. Of course, if you were given the choice between joy and pain you would choose joy every time, but when pain strikes, put up with it (the poor ancients clearly did not have the wonderful ibuprofen).

How different from the Sackler family and their mission to eliminate pain from life through drugs. If these drug peddlers had taken a more Stoic attitude, then they would never have destroyed the lives of thousands of people by getting them addicted to OxyContin. And the sensible Stoic, the wise person, if assailed by pain, doesn't take a painkiller. They take time off. If I twist my ankle playing tennis, I don't swallow opiates and battle on. That would be crazy. Instead I rest it. But what the Sackler family did was make it possible for Appalachian mine workers to carry on working even though their body was telling them to stop.

Painkillers may have their place, but it's worth bearing in mind the words of one modern-day Stoic, Penny Rimbaud, the ascetic founder of punk band Crass: 'The pain is still there. You just can't feel it.'

But even when you can feel it, the Stoic advises that you should remain indifferent to it. Epictetus includes 'chains' among a list of things to be indifferent about.

> What did you call exile, imprisonment, chains, death and dishonour in your school?
> These I called matters of indifference. They're things that lie outside the sphere of choice, and they're nothing to me.

This indifferent attitude, says Epictetus, will be a source of strength and power. Take the heroic indifference to the material world exhibited by Socrates at his trial. Epictetus ends his *Handbook* with a line from Socrates which mentions the men who brought him to trial: his accusers. 'Anytus and Meletus may kill me, but they cannot harm me.'

This is a contraction of several lines from Plato's *Apology*, where Socrates maintains that death cannot affect his *eudaimonia*.

> Neither Meletus or Anytus can do me any harm at all . . . no doubt my accuser might put me to death or have me banished or deprived of civil rights, but even

if he thinks . . . that these are great calamities, I do not think so.

By using the power of his mind Socrates proclaims supreme indifference to death. The implication is that, given the correct training, we could all do this if we chose to.

(A note on vocab: Seneca makes a distinction between two types of pain: *labor*, 'work', and *dolor*, 'pain'. In the Greek we had *ponos* and *algos*. It's fascinating that 'work' was seen as a species of pain, rather than a source of pride, as today's Calvinists would have us believe. I concur that work is a pain, and would argue with the Epicureans that it's best avoided rather than endured.)

As a final word, we might add that some people like pain. They're called masochists. They pay people to flog them. For them, pain is pleasure. Which sort of proves the Stoic point: how we react to pain is up to us.

So much for physical pain. What do the Stoics say about mental pain? How do they deal with anxiety and distress? For as medicine is the art of healing the body, so philosophy, says Cicero, is the art of healing the soul. And, he says, 'diseases of the soul are both more dangerous and more numerous than those of the body'.

Distress of the soul was a subject dear to his heart: his only daughter Tullia had recently died at the age of 33, a month after giving birth to her second son. The heartbroken Cicero wrote an essay on grief called *Consolatio*, which we'll return to.

Cicero uses the word *aegritudo*, which we would translate as distress, grief, sorrow, anxiety or melancholy. It was the avowed aim of the philosophers to remove anxiety and misery from people's lives, whatever happened to them.

Philosophy was an anti-depressive system. Epicurus had hoped to convince the people that their anxiety around superstitious beliefs was groundless, since the world was made of random atoms colliding with one another. The Stoics, by contrast, believed in providence and the *logos*, but this should also help when it came to anxiety. Since all is as it is meant to be, what's the point in worrying? It has no practical effect. Starkly put, they would argue that anxiety is a choice.

The phrase 'beside themselves' is, Cicero says, well put. Grief causes us to lose control. Medea, for example, was driven crazy over the unfaithfulness of Jason. In revenge she murdered her own children by him. But this was not wise. The wise man, the sage, says Cicero, does not yield to grief or melancholy, to mental pain or anguish. It may not be easy, he goes on, but we must wrestle with distress.

> Mental pain means decay, torture, agony, hideousness; it rends and corrodes the soul and brings it to absolute ruin. Unless we strip it off and manage to fling it away we cannot be free from misery.

The wise man, he says, has an unchanging expression on his face. He never looks miserable.

> Xanthippe used to claim that her husband Socrates always wore the same look; she said she saw him going out and returning with his countenance always unchanged . . . a calm and sunny look.

But misery is surely excusable, however wise you are, when the painful event, like a bereavement, has come as a shock. It's surely easier to bear the pain of the death of a parent who has lived to be over 80 and been dying for a while, which you have anticipated, than that of a daughter in her twenties which comes out of the blue.

Cicero uses the 'you're not the only one' method of alleviating grief. 'Attention is called to those who have lost their children by giving instances and so the sorrow of those whose grief is excessive is softened by the examples of others who have suffered.' And Marcus Aurelius insists that 'the soul wrongs itself when it is overcome by pleasure or pain', repeating the Stoic maxim that it's our reaction to events that counts, not the events themselves: 'When you are vexed at some external cross, it is not the thing itself that troubles you, but your judgement of it.'

The Greeks use the word *pathos* for a disease of the soul. *Pathos* is defined as 'a motion of the soul contrary to nature'. *Pathos* creeps in when reason is unseated.

Now, you may well be thinking: this is all pretty harsh. First you expect me to scorn physical pain, then to scorn the pain of bereavement. This is surely making me into an unfeeling robot, a Mister Spock, free from emotion and passion and therefore cold and unyielding, like a rock. Well, it is true that the avowed aim of the Stoics is to create a wise man or *sophos*: unperturbed, passionless, calm, steady and free. But I don't think the Stoics are actually heartless. No-one was saying that Cicero ought not to feel grief at the shocking death of his daughter. The point is that he used the balm of philosophy to heal his soul over time. Philosophy is therapy. I went to visit the parents of a friend of mine who died at 26, 20 years after his death. I was struck that their shelves were filled with the Stoic authors. Clearly two millennia later those severe old men still have the power to heal.

And Epictetus, for all his aggression and hard-headedness, is not lacking in human feeling. He tells the story of the man who ran away from home when his daughter was ill because he could not bear the possible outcome of death. Epictetus reprimands him for not staying at home. 'Family affection is in accordance with nature,' he says, and talks about the mother's love for her child.

As for why the Stoics matter, we can see that they do enormously as an alternative to pharmaceutical cures for mental and physical pain. I experienced severe mental pain when Elon Musk became, briefly, Governor of the Entire World. But I must learn that this is something beyond my control, and that I can be happy despite his power. Philosophy is an anti-depressant and a painkiller. Its aim is happiness, and we'll look at how to achieve that in the next chapter.

8

Happiness

The man of wisdom should have the sort of mind that would befit a god.

SENECA

To be free from anxiety, to do what you want, to live free, to float through life, to think nothing of the outrageous slings and arrows that get hurled at us on a daily basis, in short, to be happy: this is the aim of the Stoic.

The Stoics say you should live 'according to nature'. But they don't mean that you should relocate to an off-grid hut in the woods, grow kale and spear fish in the stream (though why not?). By 'nature' they mean something more like 'God', 'destiny', 'fate'. For them the idea of 'nature' is intimately tied up with their word *logos*. This very much gives the Stoics their Christian vibe: we remember the first words of John's Gospel: 'In the beginning was the Word, and the Word was with God, and the word was God.' And the word that is translated as 'word' here is *logos*. You can only live according to nature, say the Christians, if you believe in the *logos*, in divine providence. That is at the heart of everything.

Let's look at the doctrine of indifferents or *adiaphora* ('free from differences' in the Greek). While writing this book I've been reading the original Stoic texts for two or three hours every day. The message is repeated again and again. And I can testify that the idea of indifference is a powerful one. If you keep repeating it to yourself over and over, it starts to sink in. When your partner does something really annoying, like fail to flatten cardboard boxes properly for the recycling, or sigh audibly, or leave the cupboard doors open, or lose their keys, you just say to yourself, 'I am supremely indifferent!'

Things that are conventionally valued as good by society, things like wealth, good health, fame and lots of followers on social media, are considered to be indifferents by the Stoics. Not good, not bad, just indifferent. Likewise, things considered to be bad: pain, poverty, disgrace and exile. These too are indifferent. They're neither here nor there. They should be things I don't really care about. That's not to say I am against riches or honours per se. Or that I am in favour of pain and poverty. It's just that these things should not be permitted to affect my happiness.

Happiness cannot be found in external things like money, success, fame, sex and a million followers on Instagram. They may bring fleeting pleasure, but not real happiness. It is of course possible to be happy if rich or famous or both. It's just that riches and fame and lots of sex and millions of followers will not bring happiness. In the same way, poverty need not be an impediment to happiness: just look at Socrates and Diogenes. They were poor and happy. Wealth is a matter of indifference.

Remember the word the Greeks used for happiness: *eudaimonia*, 'good demon-ness'. *Eu* means 'well' or 'good' and *daimon* 'spirit' or 'divinity' or possibly 'conscience'. So we could also render it as 'well demoned', 'having a good guardian spirit', 'having a good conscience', 'wellness' or perhaps 'being in harmony with your own divine inner spark'. We could also interpret it to mean something like 'harmony of man's will with God's'. To experience *eudaimonia* means that you are successfully going with the flow. Everything is as it should be. So when a thug in the street swears at you, you just float on by, serene in the knowledge that the thug's words can only hurt you if you allow them to. The Stoics are calm in the face of what look like bad things because they believe the bad things to be part of God's plan. Like the wise Taoist, they refrain from judging things to be good or bad.

When Seneca wrote that the happy life 'is a life that is in harmony with its own nature', the phrase he used for 'happy life' was *beata vita, beatum* meaning 'blessed' or 'fortunate' (and apparently a word that Cicero invented). This is actually quite different from our word 'happiness'. As correctly outlined in Aldous Huxley's *Brave New World*, it's possible to be a happy, ignorant slave. You can be happy in the way a pig is happy when swimming in shit, stupidly happy, as we humans swim in entertainment, distracted by 'sex and TV' as John Lennon put it. That's not the kind of happiness the Stoic is seeking.

We can choose what we make of the world. It is up to us. The word the Stoics use is 'assent'. The world is made of various impressions which we receive through our senses. We still use this word today in the expression, 'I get the impression that—.' Having received these impressions, we can then choose whether or not to 'assent' to them. Sometimes we appear not to have any choice. An impression will be made on us – a thug appears – and our body will react immediately: you feel sick or your throat will tighten. But following this first involuntary reaction, you have the choice of allowing your reason to prevail. The Stoic student undertakes a years-long attempt to train themselves to develop their power of reason. It's analogous to going to the gymnasium, they say. Just as we think it's quite normal to train our bodies and get fitter, so we should spend time training our minds.

Epictetus introduces the idea of impressions at the start of his *Diatribes*. He imagines looking at something made of gold. Why do we think it is beautiful? It is our own minds that tell us so.

> For what else is it that tells us that gold is beautiful?
> The gold itself does not tell us. Clearly it is the faculty
> which makes use of external impressions.

An 'impression', then, is a message delivered to the senses by the outside world. It could be an image, a sound, a smell. The impression blasts itself at us, and then our reasonable faculty processes this impression. We see a gold bracelet and think, 'Ah, that is beautiful!' This, Epictetus tells his students, is how we drink in the world around us.

> What else judges with discernment the art of music,
> the art of grammar, the other arts and faculties,
> passing judgement on their uses and pointing out the
> seasonable occasions for their use?

Diogenes Laertius, in his essay on Zeno, puts it like this: 'An impression is an imprint on the soul.'

The Greek words here are *phantasia* for impression, *tupos* for imprint and *psyche* for soul, which is why I think this phrase sounds far more arresting in the Greek than in our rather dry translations. A more romantic rendering might go something like: 'A phantasm is a stamp on the psyche.' We're stuck, though, with the word 'impression', because of course 'fantasy' has changed its meaning over the millennia and now means something purely imaginary. But originally it meant both real and imagined impressions. Some phantasms or impressions, say the Stoics, come from the real physical world. Others are spirited up from our mind or what we would call today our imagination. The gods, say the Stoics, have given us the power of reason. We are subject to an array of phantasms and must rearrange them all. We use our will to do this.

Says Epictetus:

> The gods have put under our control only the most excellent faculty of all and that which dominates the rest, namely, the power to make correct use of external impressions.

We humans make the mistake, says Epictetus, of loading too much on our plate and worrying about the things that are not under our control.

> Although it is in our power to care for one thing only and devote ourselves to but one, we choose rather to care for many things, and be tied fast to many, even to our body and our estate and brother and friend and child and slave. As a result, being tied down to do many things, we are burdened and dragged down by them.

There are hints here of the Hindu idea of 'attachment'. We get attached to people and things, and this causes sorrow. I am given a beautiful cup. I drop it on the kitchen floor and it smashes into a million tiny pieces. This makes me sad. But I'm only sad because I became attached to the cup and because I have chosen to be sad. I could equally choose not to be sad. If I'd been indifferent to the cup, then I might have been able to bear its loss with an even temper.

So if you cultivate the doctrine of *adiaphora* or 'indifferents', the Stoics promise, then you will float around the world in a state of extreme Zen detachment. Life, says Epictetus, is like playing a ball game like tennis. Yes, when you play tennis, you try to play well and try to win. But really – it's only a ball.

Let's remind ourselves of the Stoic concept of *ataraxia*, meaning 'free from disturbance by external things'. We can compare *apatheia*, which means 'freedom from passions'. *Ataraxia* is the enviable power to stop getting annoyed by setbacks and disappointments and other people and thugs in the street and idiotic drivers at roundabouts and broken cups and Donald Trump and partners who don't close cupboard doors; in other words, the things over which you have no control.

Again, this is a matter of training. When you go to bed, run through the day in your head. Exult in the occasions when you have successfully employed your reasonable faculties to resist the outpouring of a useless emotion like anger or misery. Start with the small things. Maybe your partner didn't empty the dishwasher or left a pile of dry laundry in the hallway. A drunken teenage son climbed in through your window at four in the morning and woke you up. Or worse: on his deathbed your father decided to give your inheritance to the donkey sanctuary. Can you remain unperturbed? Can you stay *ataraxic*? Can you resist getting worked up, and treat those two imposters triumph and disaster just the same, as Kipling famously advised in his Stoic poem, 'If'?

Train yourself to be happy, agrees Seneca.

> If the body can, with training, come to such a peak of endurance that it is able to sustain punches and kicks from more than one opponent, to bear the hottest glare of the sun, the most scorching heat of the dust, and to do this for an entire day while drenched with its own blood, then surely the mind can be strengthened more easily to accept the blows of fortune, to be knocked down and trampled and get up again.

This last bit sounds like a Chumbawamba refrain, indeed.

'It is in virtue that happiness exists,' says Diogenes Laertius in his life of Zeno.

> Virtue is the state of mind which tends to make the whole of life harmonious. When a rational being is perverted, this is due to the deceptiveness of external pursuits or sometimes to the influence of associates.

After all, you can be happy with nothing, says Epictetus, and he gives his pupils the example of the Cynics and imagines one of these punky philosophers talking.

> Look at me! I am without a home, without property, without a slave; I sleep on the ground, I have neither wife nor children, no miserable governor's mansion, but only earth, and sky, and one rough cloak. Yet what do I lack? Am I not free from pain and fear,

am I not free? Has anyone among you seen me with
a gloomy face?

Who knew you didn't need slaves to be happy? I must sell mine immediately.

On the subject of *eudaimonia*, Epictetus repeats the standard Stoic tenets. Happiness comes not from without but from within.

> What is a happy life? It is security and lasting
> tranquillity, the source of which are a great spirit and
> a steady determination to abide by a good decision.
> How does one arrive at these things? By perceiving
> the truth in all its completeness, by maintaining
> orderliness, measure and propriety in one's actions,
> by having a will that is always well intentioned and
> generous, focused on rationality and never deviating
> from it, as lovable as it is admirable.

'The man of wisdom', he adds, 'should have the sort of mind that would befit a god.'

Want to be happy? Be godlike, be supremely indifferent, care not for what others care about, keep it simple. The true Stoic practises *athaumastia*, or 'freedom from surprise', 'absence of wonder', 'imperturbability'. Nothing surprises me, they say.

If that sounds like an impossible task, it is. As you've seen, Epictetus and Seneca and the rest hold up the example of 'the wise man' as our model and goal. But this state of complete wisdom or enlightenment is unlikely ever to be attained by a human being. Socrates and Diogenes of Sinope are the only ones who came close. For us mere mortals, progress is enough. We can gradually move towards a state of happiness, of living a virtuous life, according to nature. To go with the flow. We'll never get there, but we can try.

This idea of a journey is also embedded in the very word 'philosophy'. It means 'love of wisdom'. And as Socrates says, to 'love' something does not mean that we possess it. It means that we think it is lovely and would like to move towards it. The philosopher is radically humble. Socrates said he knew nothing. He contrasted the philosophers, who knew that they knew nothing, with the 'sophists' of Athens. These were the men who went around Greece teaching ambitious youth the ways of the world and getting paid for it handsomely. Think Jordan Peterson in our day. We could translate 'sophist' as 'know-it-all'. The Sophists were pleased with themselves. That is not a Stoic virtue and is highly dangerous.

So we can try to be godlike, just as I try to be Roger Federer-like when I play tennis. Of course I'm never going to get there. But I can enjoy trying. And I don't do this alone. No man is an island, and the Stoics, while they counselled radical self-sufficiency and self-reliance, and a sort of rock-like fortitude, were also social creatures, to whom friendship was at least quite important.

9

Friendship

It is a good thing to have many friends.

ZENO

Does the Stoic have mates? The Stoic message to be completely self-reliant or *ataraxic* and depend on nothing or no-one outside yourself for your happiness or *eudaimonia* might lead you to conclude that, for the Stoic school, friends are unimportant. Is the Stoic like the rock in Paul Simon's song, an island, who has no need for friendship, only books and poetry?

Well, up to a point, Lord Copper.

One of the great philosophical friendships was that of Montaigne, who was a sort of semi-Stoic, and his friend Etienne de la Boétie. Boétie was a brilliant young magistrate who in 1553 wrote a proto-anarchist, Aldous Huxley-style essay called 'On Voluntary Servitude'. He was young when he wrote it: possibly late teens or early twenties. Montaigne said that the essay was composed 'in honour of liberty against tyrants'. It was a visionary anarchistic analysis of tyranny: there is a weird magic, says de la Boétie, by which millions of people are seduced and charmed by a tyrant, despite the obvious fact that the tyrant is completely uninterested in their welfare. The people, blinded by their love for the cult leader, give up their freedom. In a Gandhiesque message Boétie recommends a quiet withdrawal from acquiescence with power.

The tyrant, Boétie, goes on, has no friends.

> The fact is that the tyrant is never truly loved, nor does he love. Friendship is a sacred word, a holy thing; it is never developed except between persons of character, and never takes root except through mutual respect; it flourishes not so much by kindnesses as by sincerity. What makes one friend sure of another is the knowledge of his integrity: as guarantees he has his friend's fine nature, his honour and his constancy. There can be no friendship where there is cruelty, where there is disloyalty, where there is injustice. And in places where the wicked gather there is conspiracy only, not companionship: these have no affection for one another; fear alone holds them together; they are not friends, they are merely accomplices.

Boétie died in 1563 at the age of 32.

In Montaigne's essay 'On Friendship' he defines two different sorts. There is the very close soulmate relationship he enjoyed with his brilliant friend. Then there are what he calls 'common friendships', normal everyday acquaintances.

The first kind of friendship, according to Montaigne, was transcendent: 'I think 'twas by some secret appointment of heaven.' They met at a party:

> our first meeting, which was accidentally at a great city entertainment, we found ourselves so mutually

taken with one another, so acquainted, and so endeared between us, that from then on nothing was so near to us as one another.

He says the friendship he went on to enjoy with Boétie was sublime. 'I know no man comparable to him,' he writes with hyperbole. 'We were halves throughout.' They were soulmates: 'Our souls mingle and blend with each other so completely that they efface the seam that joined them, and cannot find it again.'

The two men compared their bond to a celebrated friendship from antiquity: that of the older Socrates and the younger Alcibiades. Socrates was ugly on the outside and beautiful on the inside. Alcibiades was very beautiful on the outside (as for inside, that's up for debate). In this scenario, Montaigne was Alcibiades and Boétie was Socrates. This was a truly exalted union. 'Let no-one, therefore, rank other common friendships with such a one as this.'

Montaigne compares this divine connection with more prosaic relationships. 'In those other ordinary friendships, you are to walk with a bridle in your hand, with prudence and circumspection, for in them the knot is not so secure that a man may not half suspect it may slip.' He goes on to add a Stoical reflection: 'There is nothing to which nature seems so much to have inclined us, as to society; and Aristotle says that good legislators had more respect to friendship than to justice.'

Our seven Stoics, as we might expect, hold back from such displays of passion when talking about friendship. Theirs is a most rational analysis. Zeno appeared to think that since we live in a society of humans, it's good to have friends. We are sociable by nature. In his essay on the first Stoic, Diogenes Laertius says the Stoics believe that human beings should not live as hermits: 'Nor yet will the wise man live in solitude.' Friendship, or *philia*, which is a form of love, is a good thing. It's related to community.

> By friendship they mean a common use of all that has to do with life, wherein we treat our friends as we do ourselves.
>
> They argue that a friend is worth having for his own sake and that it is a good thing to have many friends.

So the wise Stoic has lots of friends. And they're all really nice, because bad people can't have friends. 'Friendship, they declare, exists only between the wise and the good.' Your friend can act almost like a *daimon* or conscience. Your friend completes you, and complements you. 'To the question, "Who is a friend?" his answer was, "A second self (alter ego)."'

The harsh Epictetus, however, is sceptical about friendship. A friendship can end quite easily, he says. Money or love or the chance of a promotion can turn friends against one another. 'Throw between you a pretty wench, and the old man as well as the young one falls in love with her; or again, a bit of glory.' He argues that our number one motivation is survival. 'Every living thing is to nothing so devoted as to its own interest.' He gives the Trojan war as an example.

> Alexander was a guest of Menelaus, and if anyone has seen their friendly treatment of one another, he would have disbelieved any man who said they were not friends. But there was thrown in between them a morsel, a pretty woman, and to win her war arose.

The 'morsel' to which Epictetus refers was of course Helen of Troy. Menelaus had been married to Helen when Alexander, also known as Paris, abducted her. I've seen this happen to my friends: one friend's wife ran away with his best mate after a year of marriage. They never spoke again. So there's something to be said for Epictetus's advice to handle friends carefully and to avoid relying on them.

Worse still, Epictetus warns that some of your so-called friends may be just using you for their own self-interest: 'How do you know that, when you have lost your utility, as that of some utensil, he will throw you away like a broken plate?'

Seneca, perhaps influenced by Epictetus, also warns his readers against 'fair-weather friends'.

> A friend taken on because of his utility will be pleasing only as long as he is useful. That is why those who are in prosperity have a crowd of friends hanging about, while those who have had a fall are deserted.

You must therefore choose your friends wisely, say the hard-headed Stoics. Boétie gives the example of Seneca, who taught Nero. But Nero turned out to be most unfriendly. He ordered Seneca to commit suicide. Serve not a tyrant, is the message. He will never be your friend.

Seneca, though, clearly loved his real friends, and talks about them a lot. One of our main sources of his Stoic wisdom are his avuncular letters to his young friend Lucilius. In letter number 9 he refutes the idea of the Stoic as a solitary rock-like thing. 'Even though the sage is content with himself, he still wishes to have a friend, a neighbour, a companion.'

It would be nice, thinks the sage, to have some friends to be sage-like with – with whom, in other words, to share your sagacity. And ideally, your friend should also be wise. Friends give you the opportunity to practise your virtue.

> He is made active by another person who is wise . . .
> He will bring him joy and strengthen his confidence,
> and each one's delight will grow from the sight of
> their mutual tranquillity.

Yes, we get virtuous with a little help from our friends. And being ataraxic, says Seneca, means that if you lose your friend, you will be able to continue to be eudaimonic.

> The wise person does have a use for friends, and wants
> to have as many as possible. But he does not want
> them in order to live a good life.
> He will do that even without friends, for the highest
> good does not look for instruments outside itself.
> He is self-sufficient, not in that he wants to be without
> a friend, but in that he is able to – by which I mean
> that he is able to bear the loss with equanimity.

Friends are nice to have, in other words. But you should not rely on them as you seek *eudaimonia*. Harsh.

The semi-holy emperor Marcus Aurelius reckoned that being a good friend was a sign of good character, recommending to the aspiring Stoic a 'readiness to do others a kindness, and eager generosity, and optimism, and confidence in the love of friends'. Be wary, though, of friends giving gifts and favours: 'to learn in accepting seeming favours from friends not to give up our independence for such things nor take them callously as a matter of indifference'.

Marcus has another nice use of friends. Just thinking about them, he says, can cheer you up when feeling miserable.

> When thou wouldst cheer thine heart, think upon the good qualities of thy associates; as for instance, this one's energy, that one's modesty, the generosity of a third, or some other quality of a fourth. For nothing is so cheering as the images of the virtues mirrored in the characters of those who live with us.

Finally he recommends creating an advisory council out of your friends. This will help guard against the kind of lonely tyranny that Boétie talks about. 'It is fairer that I should follow the advice of friends so many and so wise, than that friends so wise and many should follow my single will.'

May I close with some thoughts from St Augustine of Hippo, revolutionary North African Christian of the fourth century? Like Montaigne, he lost a very close friend when young. Their friendship, says Augustine in the *Confessions*, was 'sweet to me above all sweetness of that in my life'.

But the friend died of a fever. And I think anyone who has lost a friend when young will recognize the emotions Augustine describes. In my own case, a close friend of mine when I was 30 and he was 32. To me this friend was a Boétie. He was a brilliant journalist. It was a horrible shock, and at the time I cried non-stop for days. I didn't know where all the tears were coming from: how could the area behind the eyes hold such much water? I still sob when I think about him.

Augustine was similarly traumatized by his young friend's death.

> And at this, my heart was utterly darkened; and whatever I beheld was death. My native country was a torment to me, and my father's house a strange unhappiness . . . mine eyes sought him everywhere, but he was not granted them; and I hated all places, for they had not him; nor could they now tell me, 'he is coming', as when he was alive and absent . . . only tears were sweet to me, for they succeeded my friend, in the dearest of my affections.

Nothing could relieve his overwhelming grief.

> For I bore about a shattered and bleeding soul, impatient of being born by me, yet where to repose it, I found not. Not in calm groves, not in games and music, nor in fragrant spots, nor in curious banquetings, nor in the pleasures of the bed and the couch; nor (finally) in books or poesy, found it ease.

Here we find an insight into common remedies for depression in fourth-century Algeria. They're remarkably similar to the ones found in modern self-help books and magazines. In the end Augustine, having clearly attempted to assuage his pain by indulging in the pleasures of the bed and in curious banquetings, opted for a more drastic course of action: he moved to Carthage.

We'll return to the subject of death, and what Augustine did next, later. But now let's turn to another aspect of Stoic thought. We've mainly been looking at ethics so far, the art of how to live virtuously in the world. But the

Stoics were also interested in logic or *logikos*, and theorized about it as part of their philosophy. They reckoned that logical disputation – in other words, training the mind to spot the flatterers and the deceivers – was a very good first step on the route to philosophical fulfilment.

The study of logic could be the first step to happiness. From *logikos* comes *eudaimonia*.

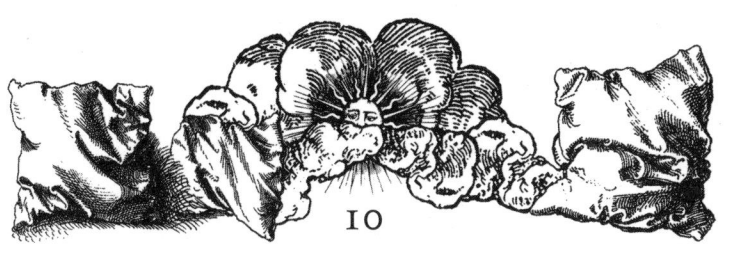

10

Logic

Philosophic doctrine, say the Stoics, falls into three parts: one physical, another ethical, and the third logical.
DIOGENES LAERTIUS

So far we've been principally interested in what you might call the ethical or 'self-help' aspects of Stoic philosophy. But in order to live well and virtuously, say the Stoics, or at least some of them, you must study logic or *logikos*. This will help to free you from believing the lies of the tyrants, and spot dissembling and bullshit, and think clearly. Your logic will help you to make a proper judgement on the *phantasia* or impressions the world blasts at you. It will enable you to tell the true from the false.

Mr Spock is a recent example of a perfectly logical being. Is he a role model?

Logic, says Diogenes Laertius, is likened by the Stoics to the shell of an egg, where philosophy is the whole egg. The white of the egg is physics and the yolk is ethics. This is a slightly baffling analogy, but I suppose you could take it to mean that logic is the means of apprehension; it's the process of sorting out your impressions or *phantasia*. The yolk is your true happy inner self, while the white is the physical world that surrounds you. Something like that.

Well. Can the study of *logikos* make you happy?

Our second Stoic, Chrysippus, was interested in logic, and came up with 'the five indemonstrables'. You could substitute X and Y for his phrases 'the first' and 'the second':

1. If the first, then the second; but the first; therefore, the second.
2. If the first, then the second; but not the second; therefore, not the first.
3. Not both the first and the second; but the first; therefore, not the second.
4. Either the first or the second; but the first; therefore, not the second.
5. Either the first or the second; but not the second; therefore, the first.

Don't worry, I'm not expecting you to get that immediately, if at all. We're not at the Bertrand Russell point of abstract logical reasoning yet. However, it is fascinating to see that the Greek thinkers were producing writings that were easily as sophisticated and abstract as John-Paul Sartre or Saussure. And on reading these lines from Chrysippus the brain starts sharpening up, even if we don't really understand what he's getting at.

A well-known logical puzzle, and in fact a playground game today, which interested the early Stoics is the statement, 'I am lying: true or false?' That also gets the brain cells ticking over, a bit like Wordle. This paradox was supposedly invented by the philosopher Eubulides, who also invented the horns paradox, where you ask the victim, 'Have you lost your horns?' Answering 'yes' or 'no' both seem absurd (unless you are on a Halloween night out and have mislaid a bit of your costume).

A third conundrum from Eubulides was called the Sorites, meaning heap. Say you have a pile of 10,000 grains of sand. If I take a grain away, do I still have a heap? Why, yes. But at which point does taking one grain away from a heap make it a not-heap? Two grains of sand is surely not a heap, and one is certainly not.

Ancient philosophers often dismissed such puzzles as childish nonsense. But as one twenty-first-century academic, Pieter A. M. Seuren, says, they're amazingly relevant today. 'Indeed, one may say that they define, more or less, the whole research programme of twentieth-century semantics.' Semantics is defined as the study of logic in language, i.e. what words really mean, and how their meaning changes according to context.

At the heart of the study of logic is the syllogism. This is defined as a three-line proof. Two statements are followed by a conclusion. Here's a simple one, composed by your author.

> Liars are bad men.
> Trump is a liar.
> Therefore Trump is a bad man.

Logic ought to make the reasoning human being realize that Trump is bad. But instead, as is often the case with tyrants, Trump tends to impress his *phantasia* on the people quite successfully, and they respond without logic and with pure *pathe*, or emotion. The Stoic, I think, would calmly assess Trump and decide not to be taken in by his seductive rhetoric.

Another syllogism might go:

Logic makes you happy.
Mr Spock is a master of logic.
Therefore Mr Spock is happy.

Trekkies will be able to tell me whether or not that one stands up to scrutiny.

Seneca came up with a nice Stoic syllogism, one which shows us how loathed gladiator managers were in ancient times. (Think of Oliver Reed in Ridley Scott's *Gladiator*.)

That which can belong to the vilest and most despicable kinds of people is not a good.
But wealth can belong to the pimp and the manager of the gladiators.
Therefore wealth is not a good.

Yep, well proved, I would say. But hang on. Surely it would be very possible for a vile and despicable man to own a good and virtuous slave? Anyway, it's always nice to hear logical condemnations of wealth, and we'll be looking at a lot more later on.

A nice, simple Stoic syllogism with an ethical flavour was created by the Stoic philosopher Posidonius (135–51 BC).

Those things which confer on the mind neither greatness nor confidence nor freedom from anxiety are not goods.
But wealth, health, and similar things do not do any of these things.
Therefore they are not goods.

We might be quite surprised, by the way, that the Stoics do not include 'health' as a 'good', since most of us would consider it to be. But then imagine the freedom that would come if you could be happy when ill or disabled. A friend of mine's octogenarian dad cannot walk, but is amazingly free of self-pity. The dad's granddaughter, aged ten, wrote a short piece for school in which she said, 'My grandfather is in a wheelchair but he doesn't mind.' A brilliant definition of Stoicism, I think!

In similar manner Zeno, the first Stoic, attempted to use syllogisms to convert his pupils to the path of righteousness. In a letter to Lucilius, Seneca gives an example.

> Zeno, who is the wisest of men . . . wished to dissuade us from drunkenness. Listen to how he proves that a good man will not become drunk:
> > No-one entrusts a secret to a man who is drunk.
> > But one does entrust a secret to a good man.
> > Therefore a good man will not be drunk.

For Seneca, though, who was sometimes snooty about syllogisms, this reasoning doesn't really work:

> In mockery of this, one could use similar reasoning to prove the exact opposite. Here's how, taking just one example:
> > No-one entrusts a secret to one who is asleep.
> > But one does entrust a secret to a good man.
> > Therefore a good man does not sleep.

But some basic logic can help in dislodging bits of received wisdom that are wrong. Musonius Rufus, who taught Seneca, is a fan of simple logical argument. He says that logic is required to begin to teach philosophical arguments, and therefore virtue. Syllogistic proofs show us truths that are not, at first sight, obviously true. He takes the example of pleasure. Pleasure is seen by the Epicureans as the highest good. But the Stoics say that if you think about it, it's actually an indifferent.

> Take for example the proposition that pleasure is not a good. At first sight we do not recognize it as true, since in fact pleasure appeals to us as a good. But starting from the generally accepted premise that every good is desirable and adding to it a second equally accepted [premise] that some pleasures are not desirable, we succeed in proving that pleasure is not a good.

Rufus argues that such proofs must be apprehended first by the intellect. Having had the truth proved to them, the pupils can then go out and act on the maxim. Therefore logic precedes ethics. Debate and argument precede behavioural change.

The philosophers were not afraid of using cold, hard logic to prove all sorts of points. Take the issue of exile. For most Romans and Greeks this was a feared punishment. It was humiliating. Sometimes the exiled person was sent to a seaside town with no cultured people. In fact, the threat of exile was sometimes couched in euphemisms such as, 'I hope you like the taste of fish!'

But the Stoics sought to use logic to prove that exile wasn't so bad after all. Musonius Rufus, for example, argues that exile

> does not in any way deprive us of water, earth, air, or the sun and the other planets, or indeed, even the

LOGIC

society of men, for everywhere and in every way there is the opportunity for association with them.

The wise man, he says, could be happy anywhere. 'Tell me, is not the universe the common fatherland, as Socrates held?'

Seems sensible. The Stoic view was that we should follow Socrates and Diogenes of Sinope and declare ourselves to be cosmopolitans, citizens of the world.

Some Stoic philosophers were only too aware, however, that an excess of logic was ridiculous. It was academic quibbling, the ancient equivalent of arguing about how many angels could fit on the head of a pin. Enjoyable, perhaps, but utterly without any utility whatsoever. In one anti-logic letter, Seneca gives an example of a silly syllogism:

'Mouse' is a syllable.
But a mouse eats cheese.
Therefore a syllable eats cheese.

'Some day I might find myself catching a syllable in mousetraps', he quips. 'What childish pranks!' He then complains, 'Is this what makes us knit our brows? Is this why we let our beards grow long? Are we pale and earnest in our teaching of *this*?' 'And so, dear Lucilius', he ends his letter, 'withdraw as far as you can from such challenges and quibbles of philosophers.'

This is a comfort to those of us who worry, as I do, that our brains are simply not equipped to think in this rigorous, logical and paradoxical fashion. And Socrates himself was not much interested in *logikos*. Or, for that matter, physics, which consisted in theorizing about the world around you: what is a star, what is matter, heliocentric or not, how far away is the moon? – that sort of thing. For Socrates it was all about ethics.

Likewise Epictetus. He warns his students against thinking that a mastery of logic makes you a philosopher, any more than wearing a long beard and cloak makes you a philosopher. At one point he even scoffs at logic as being a heap of 'little philosophic theories'. But he also says logic is required as we move towards the good life. He gives an entire lecture consisting of quibbling about quibbling (Book I, part 7). Here he tells his students that the reasoning faculties need to be trained.

> Most men are unaware that the handling of arguments which involve equivocal and hypothetical premises, and, further, of those which derive syllogisms by the process of interrogation, and, in general, the handling of all such arguments, has a bearing upon the duties of life.

Epictetus goes on to warn his young audience that getting good at logic, though necessary for the good life, may result in conceit. He complains that a master of logic will 'strut about in our presence, all puffed up'. Or as the *Viz* cartoon (m'lud, *Viz* was a popular comic of the 1980s) put it with less subtlety about one of its comic creations: 'Mr Logic: he's a pain in the arse.' There is another example in Shakespeare's highly annoying pedant Holofernes in *Love's Labours Lost*, who is given to uttering such absurd reprimands as, 'You find not the apostraphas, and so miss the accent: let me supervise the canzonet.' We at the *Idler* were perhaps a little bit guilty: for some years we ran a

Bad Grammar Award, ticking off politicians and advertisers for abuses of the language.

Certainly no-one likes a know-it-all, the person who goes around correcting other people's solecisms. Sir, what's a solecism? Oh, do pay attention! *Merriam-Webster* tells us.

> The city of Soloi had a reputation for bad grammar. Located in Cilcia, an ancient coastal nation in Asia Minor, it was populated by Athenian colonists called *soloikoi* (literally 'inhabitants of Soloi'). According to historians, the colonists of Soloi allowed their native Athenian Greek to be corrupted and started using words incorrectly. As a result, *soloikos* gained a new meaning: 'speaking incorrectly'. The Greeks used that sense as the basis of *soloikismos*, meaning 'an ungrammatical combination of words'. That root, in turn, gave rise to the Latin *soloecismus*, the direct ancestor of the English word solecism.

Logic, then, as I hope we have proved, when used logically, should lead to happiness or *eudaimonia*.

And logic, I think, is also a prerequisite of freedom, to which subject we now turn.

Freedom

> *The wise man alone is free.*
> ZENO, QUOTED BY DIOGENES LAERTIUS
>
> *Being asked what was the most beautiful thing in the world, [Diogenes] answered: 'Freedom of speech.'*
> DIOGENES LAERTIUS

In the slave-owning societies of Greece and Rome, issues of freedom were keenly felt. The slave-owning aspect is not a praiseworthy element of the ancient world (neither was its propensity to crucify vanquished enemies in the thousands). However, the slave system was not as brutal and inhuman as the one operated by Europeans in the sixteenth to nineteenth centuries. Slaves were generally captured soldiers from the losing side, or unlucky shipwreck victims. Slaves were often treated like pets and prized for their good looks and good manners. They could become teachers and valued members of the household. Pretty and handsome slaves in your entourage increased your social standing. On their master's death they might be given their freedom or manumitted (the word 'manumission' is remembered today in the name of a hedonistic nightclub in Ibiza renowned for the live sex show put on by its founders).

They were the lucky ones. There were also slaves who toiled in the silver mines of Laurion, producing the wealth of Athens. Anyway, slavery was certainly not seen as a good by the Stoic philosophers, who reflected on what Bob Marley called 'mental slavery' in his very Stoic 'Redemption Song'.

Wisdom is freedom and freedom is wisdom, say the early Stoics. According to Diogenes Laertius in his essay on Zeno,

> [The Stoics] declare that [the wise man] alone is free and bad men are slaves, freedom being the power of independent action [*autopragias*], whereas slavery is privation of the same: though indeed there is also a second form of slavery consisting in subordination, and a third which implies possession of the slave as well as his subordination. Moreover, according to them, not only are the wise free, they are also kings.

Here the Stoics make the classic distinction between 'freedom to' (autonomous action and freedom of speech) and 'freedom from' (enslavement or submission to your own *pathe* or emotions, or to an authority). The idea of the wise man being a king is perhaps an allusion to Diogenes the Cynic, who felt himself immeasurably superior to the common herd, despite (or because of) his complete indifference to things like money, status and security. This is the man who was so liberated that he would masturbate in public and then declare, 'If only I could get rid of my hunger with similar ease, just by rubbing my belly.' He had all but declared himself to be godlike, the ruler of all he surveyed. He was a cosmopolitan, a citizen of the world, a king.

The bad man in the quotation above is a slave to his *pathe* or emotions. These are mind forg'd manacles, in Blake's famous phrase, that must be cast off. In theory, then, the slave could be free and the free man could be a slave. The rich man could be in thrall to his possessions and the emotional man in thrall to his passions. Neither is in control. By contrast, the slave could be joyfully unmanacled.

That the Stoics aspired to freedom from various snares is apparent in their language. The prefix 'a', meaning 'absence of', is added to things they're not too keen on. *Apatheia* means 'freedom from passion'. *Ataraxia* means 'freedom from disturbance'. *Adiaphora* means 'freedom from difference'. *Aphobia* means 'freedom from fear'. And of course *anarchia*, anarchy, means 'freedom from authority'. Freedom, then, is a mental state rather than a physical one. (Plato warns, however, in Letter VIII, that 'too much anarchy' – *agan anarchian* – can lead to despotism and suffering.)

The Stoics' word for freedom itself, as a noun, was pretty weird. It's *eleutheria*, Ἐλευθερία. The *eleutheros* or free man is contrasted to the *doulos* or slave. Etymologically speaking, it seems to have some connection to the Greek word for 'giving birth' or 'deliver', and literally means something like 'a joyful arrival'. Zeus's second name was Eleutherios, the deliverer. The word gave its name to at least one festival. The Greeks founded a feast called Eleutheria after the Battle of Plataea in 479 BC when the Spartans crushed the Persians.

One contemporary historian tells the probably tall tale of another ancient festival called Eleutheria, a sort of Saturnalia, when the maidservants of Smyrna 'wore the adornments of free women'. The festival supposedly commemorated a military victory whereby the besieging army sent their maid servants dressed as free women into the besieged city to sleep with the soldiers, thus exhausting them, at which point the siege was easily effected.

In some mythologies Eleutheria was a goddess, the daughter of Hera and Zeus. She made an appearance on coins. And in Roman times the equivalent was of course Libertas.

For Epictetus, *eleutheria* or *libertas* was a lofty aspiration. He's fond of addressing his students, generally posh young men, as 'slaves', with the implication that they are a long way off from Bob Marley's goal of emancipating themselves from mental slavery. He says that freedom, paradoxically, consists in 'subordinating your own will to him who administers the universe'. The right question to ask, he says, is: 'How may I follow the gods in everything, and how may I be acceptable to the divine administration, and how may I become free?'

The answer? You must learn, he says, 'to desire each thing exactly as it happens'. The aim of education (*paideuthentas*) is to achieve these three things: *ataraxia*, *aphobia* and *eleutheria*: tranquillity, fearlessness and freedom [Bk II, ii]. 'Only the educated are free', he maintains. (Hence the *Idler*'s Latin slogan: *libertas per cultum*.)

Freedom, then, is going with the flow, submitting to destiny. It is not about asserting your will on others or on the world. And yes, I know what you're thinking. If everything is pre-ordained by fate, then what is the meaning of free will? Why do anything? Well: Epictetus also says that freedom is 'the right to live as we wish'. But you should wish, he adds, to live virtuously according to nature. It would be a mistake to wish to live for sex, money and luxury, because that would bring you fear and turmoil and sorrow, as experienced by Henry Hill towards the end of *Goodfellas*, when he is chased by helicopters. Free will exists in submission to fate, if that's not too much of a paradox.

The Stoics hold up the example of Socrates, who at his trial is supposed to have declared to the 500 jurors, 'Who is there in your knowledge that is less a slave to his bodily appetites than I am? Who in the world more free, – for I accept neither gifts nor pay from anyone?' This would imply that working for clients is a form of bondage. Later, when he is imprisoned and awaiting execution, he refuses to escape. Says Xenophon, 'When his companions wished to remove him clandestinely from prison, he would not accompany them.' Such was his desire to submit to his fate.

The Greek word for 'freedom of speech' is *parrhesia*, meaning 'speaking everything' or 'speak boldly', from *pan* for 'everything' and *rhema* for 'speech'. It was a philosophical or even political concept. It really meant 'critical speech', as Foucault explains in his famous essay on the subject.

> The *parrhesiastes* [practitioner of free speech] is always less powerful than the one with whom he or she speaks. The *parrhesia* comes from 'below', as it were, and is directed towards 'above'. This is why an ancient Greek would not say that a teacher or father who criticizes a child uses *parrhesia*. But when a philosopher criticizes a tyrant, when a citizen criticizes the majority, when a pupil criticizes his or her teacher, then such speakers may be using *parrhesia*.

So the wise ruler can expect to hear *parrhesia* from his advisers. An example might be the fool at the court who is allowed to speak the truth to the monarch. But when a teacher calls a pupil 'miserable little worm', or when a tyrant abuses a subject, that's not free speech, that's just bullying. In our own time, an example might be an outspoken right-wing hack on television who abuses Greta Thunberg. The hack argues that he is using free speech, whereas in fact he's just being an arsehole.

The great example of a free speaker in antiquity is our friend Diogenes. Having freed himself from the need to flatter, and become shameless, he was able to tell the truth, to stand up to power. He would spit at the rich people in the street, gatecrash parties and do nothing all day. This is because he had no need of money or status. When you depend on an employer, say for your mortgage payments, you will refrain from criticizing them, unless you are exceptionally bold. When my dad worked in Fleet Street he would sometimes contradict his boss in a meeting. The boss would simply reply, 'Neville, you do have a mortgage, I think?'

Diogenes, by contrast, needed nothing and no-one. When Alexander the Great visited him while he was living in a *pythos* (or upturned wine cask), the great ruler asked him if he could get him anything. 'Yes', replied the homeless philosopher. 'You can get out of my light.' Diogenes was a great piss-taker, a mocker. Plato held a seminar on the definition of man, at which the assembled academics came up with the phrase 'featherless biped'. On hearing about this abstraction, Diogenes killed a chicken, plucked its feathers, invaded the Academy and hurled the dead bird among the students, shouting, 'There's your "man"!'

Parrhesia is also distinguished from rhetoric, or the art of persuasive speaking. *Parrhesia* typically is bold, unvarnished, direct, whereas rhetoric is honeyed. The Sex Pistols were using *parrhesia* when they criticized the monarchy, and punk in general was a free speech movement. It did not use flashy oratorical arts. Punks shouted and swore. They were also concerned with matters of freedom. A job, said the Clash, was a form of slavery. Stiff Little Fingers accused the authorities of removing our freedoms and calling it liberty. For Diogenes and the punks, freedom was a refusal to enslave oneself to convention. Freedom came from breaking the rules of artificial society.

Socrates exemplified *parrhesia*, though he was not uncouth and possibly, like Diogenes, a bit adolescent. While others flattered the beautiful general Alcibiades, Socrates spoke the uncomfortable truth to him. He also went around Athens annoying people and urging them to live well, as he tells us in *The Apology*.

Seneca argues in Letter 104 that true freedom comes from giving up the superficially attractive things:

> We must begin by spurning pleasures; they weaken and emasculate us with their many demands, and they make us demand much of fortune. Next, we must spurn wealth: it is the recompense of slavery. We should give up gold and silver and everything else that weighs down prosperous houses. Liberty does not come for free. If you value it, you must devalue everything else.

Today social media companies have commodified the public's desire to speak freely. Elon Musk encourages what he call 'free speech', but this can sometimes morph into what someone else would call 'hate speech' or 'bullying' or, more crudely, 'being an arsehole', and social media platforms by their nature encourage the latter. The more clicks they get, and the more outrage created, the more money they get from their advertisers. They are, after all, merely tawdry ad sales scams. Thus there is no risk for the social media companies, and risk, says Foucault, was a key element of free speech in the ancient world. You were showing great courage by standing up to tyranny. What Elon Musk calls free speech often looks to me like the right to express your misery and resentment online. And Meta and the rest are in fact funded by the tyrants. That's not free speech. That's advertising.

Before turning to an often overlooked element of the Stoic school, which is its visionary mysticism, can we leave the final word on freedom to Etienne de la Boétie, the brilliant friend of Montaigne who died young? When only around 20 years old he wrote a brilliant anarchist essay on the weird nature of tyranny. He professed himself in disbelief at how readily people – and let's look at the US today – willingly submit to a tyrant, and argued, Stoically, that freedom can be taken through an act of will.

> You can deliver yourselves if you try, not by taking action, but merely by willing to be free. Resolve to serve no more, and you are at once freed. I do not ask that you place hands upon the tyrant to topple him over, but simply that you support him no longer; then you will behold him, like a great Colossus whose pedestal has been pulled away, fall of his own weight and break in pieces.

Mysticism

*But thou, O Zeus, the All-giver, Dweller in the
darkness of cloud, Lord of thunder, save Thou men
from their unhappy folly.*
CLEANTHES, *HYMN TO ZEUS*

Friends are surprised and amazed when I tell them that Stoicism had weird religious and mystical elements. They have been somehow led to believe that Stoic philosophy is simply some sort of mental trick for coping uncomplainingly with the pains of life, controlling the things you can control, and giving up the rest, and even possibly an antidote to mystical mumbo-jumbo. Its contemporary ancestor, the unromantically named cognitive behavioural therapy, avoids any mention of weird shit.

To the Western Stoic self-help writers of the modern age Stoicism is – to use an annoying and over-used word in business – your 'super-power'. American get-ahead Stoic manuals produce 250 pages of self-help advice plundered from the ancients without once mentioning God, still less ecstatic states and a surrender to the cosmic flow of life.

When it comes to what the ancient philosophers called 'physics' – that is, theories of how the world works – the

Stoics were fairly wacky. They believed in a sort of world-soul, a prime mover, a Gaia-like intelligent motivating force behind everything. 'God, intelligence, fate and Zeus are all one,' writes Diogenes Laertius of the Stoics in a passage which sounds more like something out of the *Bhagavad Gita* than the hard-headed, tough-talking Stoics of the modern Western imagination. The world was created by this Gaia-God thing:

> In the beginning all by himself he turned the entire substance through air into water. Just as the sperm is enveloped in the seminal fluid, so God, who is the seminal principle of the world, stays behind as such in the moisture, making matter serviceable to himself for the successive stages of creation.

God is in all things, then, including – or maybe especially – in sperm.

There was a prayer-like element, too. Zeno had said, 'The wise man will offer prayers and ask for good things from the gods.' And atheist Stoics might be surprised to learn that Cleanthes, Zeno's successor as head of the Stoic school, wrote a 'Hymn to Zeus', which firmly places Stoicism as a quasi-mystical and religious creed. The translation here is from 1881, so seems to have taken on something of the tone of contemporary Christian writing, with its 'thee's, 'thy's and verbs ending in '-eth'. I reproduce this chunk of it to point up the Christian vibe of Stoicism.

> Most glorious of the Immortals, many named,
> Almighty forever.
>   Zeus, ruler of nature, that governest all things
> with law,

> Hail! for lawful it is that all mortals should address Thee.
>
> For we are Thy offspring, taking the image only of Thy voice, as many mortal things as live and move upon the earth.
>
> Therefore will I hymn Thee, and sing Thy might forever.
>
> For Thee doth all this universe that circles round the earth obey, moving whithersoever Thou leadest, and is gladly swayed by Thee.
>
> Such a minister hast Thou in Thine invincible hands; – the two-edged, blazing, imperishable thunderbolt.
>
> For under its stroke all Nature shuddereth, and by it Thou guidest aright the Universal Reason, that roams through all things, mingling itself with the greater and the lesser lights, till it have grown so great, and become supreme king over all.

So God is seen here as a sort of benign motivating principle, something like our idea of 'nature'. We remember that the Stoic word often used for 'universal reason' was *logos*. It's the same odd word – obviously related to 'logic' – which we read three times at the slightly baffling beginning of John 1:1. I've mentioned it before, but now let's look at the original Greek.

Ἐν ἀρχῇ ἦν ὁ Λόγος, καὶ ὁ Λόγος ἦν πρὸς τὸν Θεόν, καὶ Θεὸς ἦν ὁ Λόγος

This translates as, 'In the beginning [*arche*] was the word [*logos*], and the *logos* was near [*pros*] God [*theon*], and God [*theos*] was the *logos*.'

Logos is a mysterious mystical concept, analogous to the idea of the 'way' discussed by the Taoists. The wise man, say the Taoists, is the one who lives his life according to the Tao, the 'way'. My friend, the late philosopher Charles Handy, liked to translate *logos* as 'the natural order of things', writing in the *Idler*,

> If you retranslate logos as 'the natural order of things', you get, 'In the beginning was the natural order of things, and the natural order of things was with God, and the natural order of things was God and there was nothing that was not in the natural order of things.'

That sounds to me like a far superior rendering. If you want to be happy – or at least, *eudaimonic* – then go with the flow, let it be, submit to the natural order of things. If you ever lose your legs, as Cat Stevens pointed out, you won't have to walk no more.

The word 'mystic' is itself Greek. It derives from *mystikon*, which meant 'connected to the mysteries' (and could be a good band name). For all their much-vaunted rationality and invention of democracy and obsession with legal process, the ancient Greeks believed in a lot of weird stuff, so we should not be surprised that the Stoic philosophers embraced mystical currents.

Stoicism is all about ethics, physics and logic, but the Greeks' religious rites were something else entirely. They were encouraged to give sacrifices to household gods in order to avert disaster. The Greeks were also afraid of portents in the sky: Epicurus tried to teach them that the world was a random collection of atoms and that the thunderbolts had no meaning whatsoever.

We've already mentioned the example of the oracle at Delphi. Here a sacred priestess sat on a tripod, surrounded by priests and muttered confusing sayings. Athenian citizens and others made pilgrimages to the temple, around 100 miles north of Athens, to sacrifice a goat and then imbibe some mystical wisdom. Diogenes Laertius claimed that no less a figure than Pythagoras drank from the fount of the oracle. 'Aristoxenus says that Pythagoras got most of his moral doctrines from the Delphic priestess Themistoclea.'

The Delphic priestess sat above a fissure in the rocks from which emerged mind-bending petrochemicals. She was, then, a glue sniffer. But she was not always particularly 'moral' in our sense of the word, advising Philip II of Macedon, 'With silver spears you may conquer the world.' Philip took this to mean that riches precede military success, so took over the silver mines and bribed opponents. Seems that the mystical prophetess was surprisingly pragmatic.

In later times, Cicero visited the oracle and was supposedly told, 'Make your own nature, not the advice of others, your guide in life.'

According to the Bible, the Stoic philosophers were quite fascinated by the preaching of St Paul. He supposedly came to Athens in 51 AD and preached in the *agora*. He accused the Athenians of worshipping a ridiculous panoply of gods. And the Athenian philosophers thought he was quite an interesting fellow. As Acts 17:18 relates:

> And some of the Epicurean and Stoic philosophers
> as well were conversing with him. Some were saying,
> 'What could this scavenger of tidbits want to say?'
> Others, 'He seems to be a proclaimer of strange

deities' – because he was preaching Jesus and the resurrection. And they took him and brought him to the Areopagus, saying, 'May we know what this new teaching is which you are proclaiming? For you are bringing some strange things to our ears; so we want to know what these things mean.'

Scholars reckon that – contrariwise – St Paul would have been influenced by the Stoics, and their idea of *apatheia* or freedom from disturbance by sinful impulses. I met Richard Harries, former Bishop of Oxford, at a party, and asked him about Stoic influence on the Christians. 'St Paul would undoubtedly have been aware of them as they were very much in the intellectual atmosphere of the first century AD,' he told me. 'Jesus, though, came from a very different culture and probably knew nothing about them.'

Having made a pilgrimage to see him when he was Master of Magdalene College, Cambridge, I put a similar question to the great intellectual cleric, Rowan Williams. 'You have Christians trying to establish their credentials in the intellectual world,' he said of the early Christians. 'They say, "Some of this might sound new, but you've heard it before, whether it's Socrates, or Stoics or Cynics. What you count as 'success' – stop and think about it. It's not what you believe."'

Sitting in the Master's Lodge next to the grand piano, Rowan quoted St Paul preaching Stoicesque sentiments: 'The fruits of the Spirit are love, joy, peace, patience, kindness, generosity, faithfulness, gentleness, self-control.'

Over 100 years after the death of St Paul we find a decidedly mystical edge to the writings of Marcus Aurelius, our seventh Stoic. He was sympathetic to the Christians, and wrote a letter to the governors of Asia forbidding outrages towards them (at least, some scholars believe he wrote the letter). He accuses their tormentors and accusers of being shown up as impious, and gives the Christians respect for their unswerving devotion to God.

> They [the Christians] indeed show the more outspoken confidence in their God, while you during the whole time of your apparent ignorance both neglect all the other gods and the worship of the ever-living one, whose worshippers, the Christians, you in fact harass and persecute to the death.

In his *Meditations* (originally titled simply 'To Himself'), Marcus places philosophy as a religious affair. Here are the last two items in his list of things to be grateful for:

> That by the agency of dreams I was given antidotes both of other kinds and against the spitting of blood and vertigo . . . And that when I had set my heart on philosophy, I did not fall into the hands of a sophist, nor sat down at the author's desk, nor become a solver of syllogisms, nor busied myself with physical phenomena.

So Marcus has a mystical belief in the significance of dreams. He also rejects the idea of philosophy as merely practical, and lists four mistaken applications of the noble science:

1. A method of getting ahead in the world [that's what the money-making sophists promised].
2. A form of escape from the world [seclusion at the author's desk].

3. A mere puzzle to be solved by logical disputation [solver of syllogisms].
4. A conjecture on how we got here and how the planets move [physical phenomena].

While these four pursuits are not immoral or wrong, they miss, according to Marcus, the real purpose of philosophy, which is to live virtuously and happily.

Socrates, our original Stoic, was not interested in any of the above list: he had no career, he did not attempt to escape the world, and he had little interest in syllogisms or indeed the physical world. But he did have a mystical bent: he went into trances and spoke with his daimon. At his trial he insisted that he was assiduous in his observance of the sacrifices and rituals expected of the Athenian citizen. He believed in the survival of the *psyche* after death. And weirdness was certainly in the culture for all Greeks: take, for example, the Eleusinian mysteries. This was a strange custom whereby initiates travelled to Eleusis from Athens and went through some sort of ritual. *Britannica* notes:

> The Greater Mysteries at Eleusis was celebrated annually in the month of Boedromion (September–October). It included a ritual bath in the sea, three days of fasting and completion of the still-mysterious central rite.

It was a sort of wellness centre for the ancient world, a *White Lotus*-style holiday, a trip to a health farm.

So philosophy could certainly involve intensive meditation and a sense of spiritual connection. But the Stoics also lived in the real world, and have much to say on the thorny subject of money.

13

Money

Which Seneca and other clerks maintain.
Whoso will be content with poverty,
I hold him rich, though not a shirt has he.
 CHAUCER, *THE WIFE OF BATH'S TALE*
Thou madest self-sufficiency thy rule,
Eschewing haughty wealth, O godlike Zeno!
 ZENODOTUS THE STOIC

In a letter to Lucilius (no. 87) Seneca boasts about his simple living. Just the other day, he says, he had a very basic picnic in the woods with a friend, Maximus. No fancy restaurants or cooks for them. They had barely any help, he says, 'just a few slaves – what a single carriage has room for'.

So Seneca's idea of a frugal lunch involves taking a wagon and five or six unpaid cooks and washers-up with you. I can almost see the photos in *Tatler*.

Seneca's biographer Emily Wilson says that Seneca's 'minimalist retinue' would have included

> a secretary or secretaries to note down his thoughts, as well as a doctor to tend to the master's constant

ailments, the little boy to act as his physical trainer
and jogging companion, others to wash, massage and
dress him . . .

We may chortle at Seneca's Marie-Antoinette-like tone deafness, and indeed many did at the time. Never was there so great a gap, people said, between the theory and the practice of Stoicism, as was the case with Seneca. He was hugely wealthy thanks to his money-lending operations, yet counselled poverty: a champagne Stoic.

However, such accusations of hypocrisy actually miss the point. We should look at whether or not the prescriptions and ideas make sense, not at whether or not their promoter actually lived by them. After all, we are frail, we are weak, and many of us fail to live up to our own precepts. This doesn't mean the precepts themselves are faulty. Another classic example is John Lennon, who urged his readers to imagine no possessions while playing a grand piano in a mansion. Some will call him a hypocrite; others will take heed of the message itself despite the wealth of the singer.

And a rejection of luxury living and greed was a key precept of Stoic ethics. In fact, we may say it was an obsession. Then as now, the philosophers argued that riches do not make you happy. But then as now, wanting to be rich was extremely common. Money was power. The tyrants of the ancient world, like Trump in ours, were massively wealthy. The funny thing is, I suppose, that however often over the millennia this obvious truth – money doesn't equal happiness – has been pointed out by philosophers, poets and clerics, the majority of people still lust after money. Hence lotteries, advertising and the immense suffering and *ponos* that people put themselves through for the sake of lucre.

However, that's also not to say that the philosophers who walked the walk were not more admirable than the mere spouters of doctrines. The Stoic icons as far as an embrace of poverty went were our old friends Diogenes, who loudly advertised his trampy way of living, and the great Socrates, who had a fairly normal family life but lived on little and certainly showed no love for money. As mentioned previously, he wore a threadbare cloak and went around without shoes. He famously said, on surveying the thousands of bottles of olive oil and other stuff on sale in the market at Athens, 'What a lot of things I don't need!'

The first Stoic, Zeno, also set a good example. He was perhaps a little puritanical and monk-like, though not as ascetic as Diogenes of Sinope, who made poverty into a piece of performance art. Diogenes Laertius says of Zeno,

> He used to eat little loaves and honey and to drink
> a little wine of good bouquet. He rarely employed
> men-servants; once or twice indeed he might have
> a young girl to wait on him in order not to seem
> a misogynist.

An equal opportunities employer, then. Diogenes Laertius goes on to accuse him of being miserly. 'He was very niggardly too, clinging to meanness unworthy of a Greek, on the plea of economy.'

A comic poet of the day, says Diogenes Laertius, teased Zeno for preaching poverty. He quotes:

> This man adopts a new philosophy.
> He teaches to go hungry: yet he gets
> Disciples. One sole loaf of bread his food;
> His best desert dried figs; water his drink.

We can see shades of Christ in these lines. Zeno was a byword for frugality; the phrase 'more temperate than Zeno' became a proverb. Figs, too, make an appearance as a symbol of simple living.

A key concept for the Stoics was *autarkia*, which is normally translated as 'self-sufficiency', though it's nothing to do with growing your own vegetables. It means that you are able to stand on your own two feet and avoid servility, like Socrates. Freedom is more important for *eudaimonia* than money. *Autarkia einai pros eudaimonian*, wrote Zeno: 'Self-sufficiency is all you need to be happy.' Happiness comes when you are free to say what you want and do what you want. And *autarkia* is necessarily mixed up with frugality. Luxury enslaves. In Cicero's words, virtue is all that is needed to live happily or *beate vivendum*. Riches are beside the point.

Musonius Rufus likewise praised frugality. 'One can drink from earthenware cups which are quite as good at quenching the thirst as goblets of gold.' This is clearly not a manual for living that Elton John has subscribed to. Rufus also maintained that the purpose of food was not pleasure but mere fuel. He admired the Spartans, who lived lives of strict self-denial. 'I think first of Lycurgus, who drove extravagance out of Sparta and substituted frugality.' Luxurious living, he said, 'destroys both body and soul, causing weakness and impotence in the body and lack of self-control and cowardice in the soul'.

However, he didn't appear to think that we should all live in an upturned wine jar or throw away your one remaining wooden bowl like Diogenes the Cynic. Rufus has one nice essay which explores the question of the appropriate way of making a living for the philosophically minded person. He comes up with 'farmer'.

For the earth repays most justly and well those who cultivate her, returning many times as she received and furnishing an abundance of all the necessities of life to anyone who is willing to work.

That may be a romantic view of the life of a smallholder (I tried it; it's tough). But the theory seems nice. I foresee a trend for peasant-philosophers, constructing syllogisms in the morning and hoeing the vegetables after lunch. It's a way of life embraced by the punk collective Crass, who combine art and philosophy with a high level of self-sufficiency on their one-acre farm in Essex. And it's one that Coleridge dreamed of too. When he was a young man living in Bristol, he and his mate Southey planned a philosophical commune 'on the banks of the Susquehanna' in Pennsylvania. 'When Coleridge and I are sawing down a tree', Southey fantasized, 'we shall discuss metaphysics; criticize poetry when hunting buffalo and write sonnets whilst following the plough.' I'd advise Southey to concentrate on the job in hand: buffalo-hunting and tree-sawing require a considerable focus. Multi-tasking in the way he foresees is bound to result in botched ploughing, sawing and hunting. Predictably, perhaps, the scheme came to nothing.

Returning to Seneca, he admits that though he ventures forth in a simple carriage, in order to make a statement, he is still faintly embarrassed by it. Today it's not carriages, it's cars that are the status symbols. To rebel against what I considered to be an absurd servility to the advertisers of expensive motor cars, I used to drive a 15-year-old Vauxhall Cavalier, and I was proud of my statement against consumerism. However, I confess to feeling slightly embarrassed if I arrived at a wedding and saw the car park full of smart Teslas, BMWs and Range Rovers. 'He who blushes in a shabby carriage will boast of an expensive one,' Seneca writes. 'It's only a little progress I have made so far. I do not dare wear my frugality out in the open.'

He goes on to quote the mutterings of ordinary people about those who appear to be rich, but are in fact drowning in debt. Most of us will see an echo here with present-day financiers.

> 'His property is extensive, but so too are his debts.'
> 'No-one turns out a more splendid retinue, but he does not pay his bills.'

In contrast, Seneca praises the simple-living Cato the Elder, who

> used to ride a packhorse; one laden with saddlebags, in fact, so as to carry useful articles along with him. I only wish there could be a meeting on the road between him and one of these well-heeled young squires preceded by his runners, his Numidian slaves, and a great cloud of dust.

Which reminds us of that noted well-heeled young squire P Diddy Combs, whose arrival at a function would be preceded by his runners and a great cloud of perfume, though he didn't go as far as Numidian slaves. (But he did allegedly indulge in sex marathons worthy of Caligula.) Compare that vain, showy and determinedly non-Stoic rapper to the late, great José Mujica, former president of Uruguay, who donated his entire salary to charity, lived in a simple shack in the woods and drove an old Volvo.

'If you don't have many possessions then you don't need to work all your life like a slave to sustain them,' Mujica told the *New York Times*. 'Fight for happiness, not just for wealth.' Well-heeled young squires, take note!

The Stoic way is to embrace the philosophical life. But young Lucilius says he can't afford to sit around doing nothing. So Seneca advises him to experiment with poverty, as frugality and time for thinking go together. Have a 'poor day', he suggests.

> If you want to have time for your mind, you must either be poor or resemble the poor. Study cannot be beneficial without some concern for frugality, and frugality is just voluntary poverty. So away with your excuses! 'I don't yet have enough; once I reach that amount, I shall devote my whole self to philosophy.' . . . designate certain days when you part from your own property and make scarcity your companion. Begin to have dealings with poverty.

Again, you and I are acutely aware that short periods of voluntary poverty for rich people are quite different from the misery of being really poor and in debt. However, we can also accept that voluntary poverty and the philosophical life go together like a horse and carriage. Just look at Buddha, Gandhi, St Francis, Socrates and Christ himself. My own father gave away his worldly possessions when he was 50 years old and devoted himself to a life of contemplation.

When it comes to money, the Stoics once again look a bit Christian. The early desert fathers, after all, condemned greed. And riches do not bring leisure and liberty. They bring more responsibilities.

If you have schooled yourself in deprivation, you will never be scared of it. That is the point of fasting. Ramadan is designed to extend your sympathies to the poor, to practise poverty.

Rich people take on far too many financial obligations. They buy second or even third homes, they extend their mortgages, they employ staff, they buy silly cars on hire purchase, they increase their outgoings to an absurd extent. This makes them worried: if I lose my job, then I won't be able to pay my mortgage. Thus morality is turned upside down. Like Greg and Tom in *Succession*, they will do anything to keep their job and their high income. They will lie, steal, sack people, abandon friends . . . and even allow people to die. I'm constantly astonished by people's greed. A slightly newer and bigger car or a fractionally posher ski resort or a house half a mile closer to the centre of the city appears to them more important than friendship, peace of mind or time spent with their own children. They will do anything to get these spectacularly unimportant things.

Epictetus was clear. 'When you are shown money', he asked his students, 'have you practised giving the proper answer, namely, that it is not a good thing?' He also said to them, 'Come, what says Diogenes about poverty, death, hardship?'

The wise person, whether rich or poor, or of the middling sort (like your author), lives modestly. This way he does not excite envy in others, and he lives without fear of losing it all.

Money to the wise person is an indifferent. You can be happy with it or without it. The Stoic scorns its empty promises. When assailed by the demon greed, simply say to yourself, 'I am supremely indifferent to the dubious seductions of riches.' I am *adiaphoric*. And what a great power indifference could be! It's not a reaction that is encouraged by the modern world. The ubiquitous Facebook invented the 'like' and 'dislike' buttons. These have encouraged the world to see things as good or bad. I love Trump. I hate Trump. Which, when you think about it, is a sort of madness. A philosophical social media company of the future would add an 'indifferent' button. We should all be more indifferent, and refrain from judgement, and just wait. Indifference is power.

And how can the Stoics remain so magnificently *adiaphoric* no matter what happens to them: ill-health, death, poverty, losing a limb? It's because they believe in fate . . .

14

Fate

Omnia adversa exercitationes putat.
'All his adversitie he counts mere training.'
SENECA, *ON PROVIDENCE*

When Cicero's beloved daughter Tullia died at only 33 he was heartbroken. He was so grief-stricken that he divorced his second wife Publilia for her unfeeling, uncaring reaction to the death. Says Plutarch,

> His friends came together from all quarters to comfort Cicero; but his grief at his misfortune was excessive, so that he actually divorced the wife he had wedded, because she was thought to be pleased at the death of Tullia.

But instead of merely raging at the world, he decided to sit down and solace himself with philosophy, and retired to one of his villas where he wrote an essay on fate called *De Fato*.

The Latin word *fatum* literally meant the spoken word of Jupiter, as in 'the unalterable will of heaven'. The *fata* were the three goddesses who controlled the destinies of people and cities. In Greek mythology these fates were called the Moerae, meaning 'shares' or 'portions', and again there were three: Atropos, Clotho and Lachesis. Between them they spun man's destiny.

Now before we look at *De Fato*, can I point out that there's a very good philosophical reason why the Stoics can remain calm when things are going badly (or what we call badly)? It's not just a character test. It's because they have a deep belief in Providence, in the will of the gods, in destiny, in the divine *logos*, the universal nature, the way. Losing, winning, pleasure, pain: it's all the same.

In short, the Stoics believed in fate.

And the Stoic thinking on fate is diametrically opposed to the attitude towards destiny of the rival school, the Epicureans. These pleasure-loving philosophers had a materialistic view of the universe. Taking their lead from Democritus, who had proposed the theory of atoms, they reckoned that the world was more or less the result of random collisions of atoms. This was called the 'swerve'. This is not to say that they were thoroughly atheistic, as has sometimes been asserted. They did in fact believe in some sort of divine presence or gods. But these Epicurean gods didn't really do much. They lazed around.

It's the Epicurean view of the universe that lies at the heart of Marxism: men's systems are at fault, Marx argues, and they can be changed. There is nothing inevitable about anything. Marx had studied Epicurus and his predecessor, Democritus, the atomist, for his doctoral dissertation, which he called 'The Difference Between the Democritean and the Epicurean View of Nature'. Do not put up with the outrageous slings and arrows, he argued. Oppose them.

The essay was a celebration both of these early philosophers' attack on superstition and their materialist idea that the atom was the indivisible unit that made up the world. As Marx put it in grand style,

> When human life lay grovelling in all men's sight, crushed to the earth under the deadweight of religion whose grim features lowered menacingly upon mortals from the four quarters of the sky, a man of Greece was first to raise mortal eyes in defiance, first to stand erect and brave the challenge. Fables of the gods did not crush him, nor the lightning flash and growling menace of the sky . . . Therefore religion in its turn lies crushed beneath his feet, and we by his triumph are lifted level with the skies.

The man of Greece was Epicurus. Philosophy, says Marx, not religion, should be our guide through the world.

The Stoics, by contrast, submit to God's plan. Epictetus is fond of quoting the earlier Stoic Cleanthes, teacher of Chrysippus, who said, 'Lead me Zeus, and you, Fate, wherever you have ordained for me. For I shall follow unflinching.' This means that when something apparently bad happens – someone shouts at you in the street, you break a cup, you lose a friend – it's not really bad. It's part of the plan, the *logos*, God's will. It's all meant to be. That's why Stoics can remain unperturbed and indifferent whatever befalls them. Says Seneca, 'Fate guides us . . . What is a good man's role? To surrender to fate.' And Marcus Aurelius wrote, 'You must . . . welcome all that happens, even if it seems harsh, because it leads to the health of the universe, the welfare and well-being of Zeus.'

This was the difficult task Cicero set himself in *De Fato*: to welcome all that happens. This knotty essay was written only 150 years after the death of Chrysippus, and before any of our final four Stoics got writing. The conceit of the piece is that it's a Socratic dialogue between the chatty orator Cicero and his mate Hirtius, a former consul, which takes place at Cicero's villa at the busy port of Puteoli, or Pozzuoli, in the Bay of Naples.

At the time Puteoli boasted a gigantic amphitheatre seating around 50,000 people, complete with underground passages, trapdoors and cages for animals, the likes of which you may have seen in *Gladiator 2*. Cicero, though, had removed himself from the hurly-burly and, so he says, devoted himself to discussions of philosophy and how to bring peace to the world. The Roman world was reeling from Caesar's assassination in 44 BC, just a year after the death of Tullia. Men, he says, were cooking up all sorts of mischief in the wake of this huge event. So Cicero had both private and public reasons for retreating from public life and indulging in abstract thought instead.

The orator, who sometimes calls himself an Academic rather than a Stoic, but certainly had Stoic tendencies, makes an attempt to reconcile fate with free will. He begins by rejecting the notion that random occurrences in nature have some sort of significance. He says it's ridiculous to argue, for example, that a piece of rock in a cave was fated to fall on a hero's head. That piece of rock would have fallen anyway. 'What is the point of harping on fate, when everything can be explained by nature and fortune without bringing fate in?'

Cicero also argues that though human beings may be born with a certain character, which is related to their environment and their upbringing, they can change habits through a force of will. Nature can be improved by nurture.

> Do we not read how Socrates was stigmatized by the 'physiognomist' Zopyrus . . .? He said that Socrates was stupid and thick-witted because he had got hollows in the neck above the collarbone . . . he also added that he was addicted to women, at which Alcibiades is said to have given a loud guffaw!

The point here is that Socrates had become wise and strong through the study of philosophy. He was not necessarily born that way. He overcame his nature by 'will, effort and training', in Cicero's words. (The guffaw of Alcibiades relates to the fact that Socrates, though married, was known for fancying boys, a sort of 'bear' of his day.)

Believing in fate, for Cicero, is not an excuse to give up. He mentions the 'lazy man argument', or *argos logos* in Greek, meaning 'the lazy way'. Anyway, the *argos logos* argued that if everything is predetermined, then what is the point in making any effort at all? If I am going to die, why bother calling the doctor? *Argos logos* would mean that nothing is in our power. But clearly some things are within our power. Doctors can help us to get well. 'Nor will we be blocked by the so-called "Lazy Argument". If we gave in to it, we would do nothing whatever in life.' In *De Fato* Cicero goes on to say that

> All fallacies of this sort are refuted in the same way. 'You will recover, regardless of whether or not you call the doctor,' is fallacious. For it is just as much fated for you to call the doctor as for you to recover.

Cicero goes on to praise the view on fate that the Stoic Chrysippus put forward. There had traditionally been two opposing views among philosophers.

> On the one hand, the opinion of those who deemed that everything takes place by fate in the sense that this fate exercise the force of necessity – and on the other hand the opinion of those who held that the movements of the mind are voluntary and not at all controlled by fate.

Chrysippus, says Cicero, 'stood as unofficial umpire and wished to strike a compromise'. He says that fate exists but so does free will. The Stoic master then goes on to use an Oasis-like metaphor and urges his readers to 'roll with it', while acknowledging that someone has to set the rolling thing rolling in the first place.

> In the same way therefore as a person who has pushed a roller forward has given it the beginning of motion, but has not given it the capacity to roll, so a sense-presentation when it impinges will it is true impress and as it were seal its appearance on the mind, but the act of assent will be in our power.

Fate, then, is a sort of trigger. It does not compel our actions.

Cicero concludes his essay by mocking the Epicurean idea of the 'swerve', the random collision of falling atoms which lead to an absurd world. 'Do the atoms cast lots among them which is to swerve and which not?'

All very enlightening, but the modern reader wishes that Cicero had been a little more Sappho-like and added some personal reflections on the death of Tullia to these abstract and somewhat dry reflections.

On 7 December 43 BC, Cicero met his own fate when he was assassinated on Marc Antony's orders by a centurion called Herennius. He was 63.

Some 100 years later, in around 64 AD, a year before his own grisly death, Seneca weighed in on the subject of fate and free will. He wrote a letter to Lucilius with the snappy title *Quare bonis viris multa mala accidant, cum sit providentia* ('Why do misfortunes happen to good men, if providence exists?'), generally shortened to *De Providentia* or On Providence. He was thinking about legacy: life is going to be over soon, so I'd better assure myself a place in the history books by writing some philosophy, like Cicero did.

Seneca believes in providence, destiny, fate. He thinks that the seemingly random movements of the natural world in fact have a purpose.

> Even those phenomena which seem irregular and undetermined – I mean showers and clouds, the stroke of crashing thunderbolts and the fires that belch from the riven peaks of mountains, tremors of the breaking ground . . . do not happen without a reason [*sine ratione*].

As for bad things happening, he takes the view that the word 'bad' is simply not in the enlightened Stoic's dictionary.

> You ask, 'Why do many adversities come to good men?' No evil can befall a good man; opposites do not mingle. Just as the countless rivers, the vast rain

> from the sky and the huge volume of mineral springs
> do not change the taste of the sea, do not even modify
> it, so the assaults of adversity do not weaken the spirit
> of the brave man [*viri fortis*].

Here we see the appeal of the Stoic creed to Spartanesque soldiers, Roman tough guys and so-called strong men today. Seneca reckons that God – or fate – or the *logos* – is like a stern but loving father. God makes life tough for those he loves the best. Socrates was poisoned and Cato, the avowed enemy of Caesar, Pompey and Crassus, committed suicide.

Good luck, says Seneca, is in fact bad luck. It enfeebles. 'It excites the brain, it evokes vain fancies in the mind, and clouds in deep fog the boundary between falsehood and truth.' It's true: good luck can turn you into an awful person. Just look at those American tech CEOs who are convinced that their success is a result of their unusual brilliance rather than being lucky.

Epictetus says that we're quite happy to remain cool and detached when it comes to the misfortunes of others, but less likely to be, erm, philosophical, or fate-believing, about bad things when they happen to us.

> When some other person's slave-boy breaks a drinking
> cup, you are instantly ready to say, 'That's one of the
> things that happen.' Rest assured that when your own
> drinking cup gets broken, you ought to behave in
> the same way that you do when the other man's
> cup is broken.

He takes the point further and says that you ought to be able to bear the death of a child with equanimity too.

Some other person's wife or child has died and you say, 'Such is the fate of man.' Yet when a man's own child dies, the cry is, 'Alas! Woe is me!'

Yes, I know, the Stoics could be pretty harsh. Most of us would argue that there is a difference between a drinking cup and a child. But Epictetus reckons we should accept everything that happens without judgement. It is all meant to be. *Que sera sera*.

In this the Stoics were very Taoist (and strangely, Taoism, like Buddhism, was getting going at around the same time in human history). In the *Discourses* Epictetus maintains:

> Whenever you find fault with Providence, only consider and you will find that what happens is in accordance with reason.

The word used for 'providence' here is *pronoia*, or 'foreknowledge', and the word for 'reason' is our old friend *logos*, or 'the way'.

Epictetus goes on to say that it's absurd to be jealous of another person's riches, because we would never want to do whatever he did to get rich in the first place. Again we see the characteristic Stoic mix of mystical currents and hard-headed practicality.

Of the mystical currents, it may be worth emphasizing that for the Stoics, the whole world is interconnected. 'Chrysippus says that fate is a certain natural everlasting ordering of the whole,' noted the writer Gellius: 'one set of things follows on and succeeds another, and the interconnection is inviolable.'

I daresay we're all still mightily confused on this issue. I sometimes feel I am wandering into a maze, like the Stoic philosophers in *Paradise Lost*.

> Others apart sat on a Hill retir'd,
> In thoughts more elevate, and reason'd high
> Of Providence, Foreknowledge, Will and Fate,
> Fixt Fate, free will, foreknowledg absolute,
> And found no end, in wandring mazes lost.
> Of good and evil much they argu'd then,
> Of happiness and final misery,
> Passion and Apathie, and glory and shame,
> Vain wisdom all, and false Philosophie.

We'll be hearing more from the Puritan poet in our next chapter. So let's get off our 'Hill' and come down to earth with a look at seven classic arguments against Stoicism, one in John Milton and one from another great John, Elton. So join me as we journey from the Miltonic to the Eltonic.

15

Objections

> *The philosophers ... do not have true piety, that is, the true worship of the true God, from which all the duties of leading a good life must be drawn.*
> ST AUGUSTINE, LETTER 155

Right from day one critics, commentators and wags proposed objections to the Stoic creed. You may well have been ruminating on a couple. Let's outline seven of them.

THE SHOEMAKERS' OBJECTION

A key element of the Stoic creed is frugality. We saw earlier how Socrates remarked, 'What a lot of things I don't need!' when he was in the marketplace. Diogenes threw away his one remaining possession, a wooden bowl, exclaiming, 'What an absurd encumbrance!' Again and again the Stoic writers, whether they are poor like Epictetus or rich like Seneca, encourage their readers to shun luxury, consumerism, possessions. And this shunning of the material world continues of course in Christianity and Hinduism. The whole point of a monk is that he lives and dresses simply and has few wants. It's called asceticism.

But right from the beginning, the wits of the day were keen to argue that frugality is not necessarily advisable in a market economy. We hear from Diogenes Laertius that Socrates, who went about barefoot, was teased by a comic poet called Ameipsias: 'Your sorry plight is an insult to the cobblers.' In a world where everyone was frugal, the argument would go, what would happen to the artisans and tradesmen? People who buy stuff keep the people who make stuff employed. After all, who pays the stonemasons to build the temples?

The argument persists today: do we agree with the politicians and the bankers who believe that growth and spending and the economy are the most important things in the world? Or do we retreat from the consumer economy, grow our own cabbages and dress in rags? This latter tendency is expressed in the 'degrowth' movement, which argues that a world based on unlimited growth will one day explode as its resources are in fact finite. The degrowthers are perhaps the inheritors of the Stoic legacy. They believe that not only does frugality lead to wisdom, but also consuming less will save the planet. The creed of reckless consumption and accumulation is damaging not only to the soul but also to the earth itself, which will burn up unless we change our ways. Imagine no possessions, a brotherhood of man.

THE ELTONIC OBJECTION

Elton John is not a promoter of the ascetic creed. In *Me*, Elton's excellent autobiography from 2019, the singer defends his shopping habit.

> I've always found collecting things oddly comforting and I've always enjoyed learning about things

by collecting them, whether that's records or photographs or clothes or art. I'm just lucky enough to have the money to pursue my passions further than most people. I earned that money by working hard, and if people think it is excessive or ridiculous, then I'm afraid that's their problem.

Elton does not defend his hyper-consumerism on the grounds of 'trickle-down' economics, or because it gives work to the artisans. He defends it because he finds it fun and therapeutic. He is an apostle of what is called the 'hedonic' or hedonistic society. Later he says that his friend John Lennon, though professing the renunciation of possessions in 'Imagine', was also in fact a shopaholic.

> John and Yoko were as bad as me when it came to shopping. The various apartments they owned in the Dakota were so full of priceless artworks, antiques and clothes that I once sent them a card, rewriting the lyrics to 'Imagine': 'Imagine six apartments, it isn't hard to do, one is full of fur coats, another's full of shoes.'

Possibly excessive, but in a free world, argues Elton, John and Yoko are allowed to splash their cash, even while telling others to renounce all material goods. And they must have been loved by the shoemakers and furriers.

We find support for the Eltonic objection in a possibly unlikely place: a poem by the Puritan John Milton. In 'Comus', written in 1634, when Milton was just 25, the eponymous hero mounts a spirited attack on the Stoic and

Cynic rejection of consumerism. No-one should listen to the poverty-praising philosophers:

> COMUS. O foolishness of men! that lend their ears
> To those budge doctors of the Stoic fur,
> And fetch their precepts from the Cynic tub,
> Praising the lean and sallow Abstinence!
> Wherefore did Nature pour her bounties forth
> With such a full and unwithdrawing hand,
> Covering the earth with odours, fruits, and flocks,
> Thronging the seas with spawn innumerable,
> But all to please and sate the curious taste?

Comus, the Greek god of revelry, has a slightly different argument from Elton's. It's religious. Why, asks Comus, Greek god of revelry, would nature pour forth her bounties if she didn't want man to enjoy them? Frugality is an act of impoliteness towards God. His arguments are addressed to the young heroine of the poem. He goes on to ridicule the notion of simple living. Eating lentils and drinking water is a pretty spiritless way to carry on, he says, and what's more, is disrespectful to our creator.

> If all the world
>   Should, in a pet of temperance, feed on pulse,
>   Drink the clear stream, and nothing wear
> but frieze,
>   The All-giver would be unthanked, would
> be unpraised,
>   Not half his riches known and yet despised.

Milton, in fact, goes on to recommend virtue and to reject Comus's arguments in the poem. He comes down on the side of temperance, *sophrosune*, or σωφροσύνη. And he argues, like the Stoics, that happiness comes from within, not from externals.

> He that has light within his own clear breast
> May sit i' th'centre, and enjoy bright day:
> But he that hides a dark soul and foul thoughts
> Benighted walks under the mid-day sun;
> Himself is his own dungeon.

But we've got to admit that he makes the Eltonic arguments pretty forcefully and seductively. (And so do advertisers.) But in weighing up the Eltonic argument, bear in mind that just a few pages after Elton's defence of excessive consumption, at the age of only 28 and with number ones all over the world he decides to commit suicide, so swallows a load of Valium and jumps into the swimming pool. Clearly the shopping therapy wasn't really working. It had not led to *eudaimonia* for Elton.

THE EXCESSIVELY HARSH OBJECTION

It's all very well, you Stoics parading before us an ideal of complete imperturbability in the face of mishap, disaster, bad luck, bereavement, torture, enslavement and imprisonment. But you would surely be inhumane and cold if you failed to shed a tear on the death of your husband or son. The ideal Stoic is too rock-like and aloof.

This is how Seneca puts it in his essay *On Mercy*.

> I am aware that among the ill-informed the Stoic sect is unpopular on the ground that it is excessively harsh

(*duram*) and not at all likely to give good counsel to
princes and kings; the criticism is made that it does
not permit the wise man to be pitiful, does not permit
him to pardon.

'What kind of a theory is it', he goes on, 'that bids us
to unlearn the lesson of humanity and closes the surest
refuge against misfortune, that of mutual aid?'

These objections, says Seneca, are based on a misunderstanding of the creed. Stoics are not unbending, harsh and lacking empathy, he explains. In fact, they're full of compassion. They aim to remain unruffled because that will mean they're better able to help others.

> The fact is, no school is more kind and gentle, none
> more full of love to man and more concerned for
> the common good, so that its avowed object is to be
> of service and assistance, and to regard not merely
> self-interest, but the interest of all . . . The wise man
> will come to the rescue of the distressed.

THE PERFECTION OBJECTION

This objection is a common one. OK, I want to be a Stoic. It would be nice to be able to remain unruffled no matter what happened to me. But look, it's not humanly possible. Maybe Socrates and Diogenes and Cato the Younger got there. There is no hope for weak, feeble, flawed me.

Seneca addresses this objection head on, and concludes that no-one is really expecting you to be a super-sage. He admits that truly enlightened ones are exceedingly rare. 'He is born once every five hundred years, like the Phoenix.' Maybe Socrates, Christ, Buddha, Mohammed, Bob Dylan. Really not many. (My friend John Lloyd of *QI* says that in the history of the world, only 14 people can be considered to be enlightened.) He says that this true sage is followed by three levels of Stoic – something like the belts in judo or magic users in Dungeons and Dragons. Here are Seneca's definitions of each level. I wonder where you would place yourself?

- *Level One Stoic*: 'Those who have made the most progress have got beyond the infirmities, but they still experience emotions, even though they are very near perfection.'
- *Level Two Stoic*: 'The second category comprises those who have put aside both the worst of the mind's failings and the emotions, but not in such a way as to have a secure grasp on their tranquillity: they are still liable to relapse.'
- *Level Three Stoic*: 'They have escaped greed, but still experience anger; they are not troubled by lust, but are still subject to ambition. They no longer experience desire, but they still experience fear . . . they are unconcerned about death but still terrified of pain.'

The gentle Seneca reckons that any progress towards sagehood – at all – is good. 'It is sufficient achievement to us if we are not among the worst,' he writes. He's right, I suppose. Even the occasional glimpse of level three would be quite thrilling for most of us. Can you think of anyone you know who would qualify as a Level One Stoic?

My own father has been practising something a bit like Stoicism for 40 years. It's called Raja Yoga. He lives at a retreat centre, meditates daily and aims to master the passions. He renounced all possessions, is celibate, teetotal and vegetarian, and views the world with total detachment. But progress has been slow. As my brother observes, 'Forty years of meditation, spiritual study and contemplation on the infinite nature of the soul has not made one jot of difference to our Dad's inability to lose graciously at Monopoly.' I'd say that my Dad has only reached Level Three. But maybe that's better than nothing.

THE POETIC OBJECTION

In a world of perfect Stoics, no-one would be miserable. But then there would be no need to create tragedies or any kind of art. There would be no Hamlet, no *Godfather* trilogy, no Sylvia Plath. Stoicism is sterile, boring, uninspiring. Tragic plays are watchable because they are all about a failure to be Stoic. Who would want to watch a play in which all the characters are serene, tranquil, free from passion and grin smugly as they go about their sober Stoic business in their dull-coloured clothes? Tolstoy may have ultimately failed to find happiness, but he wrote some excellent books. Happiness does not always make for great art.

I put a similar objection to Rowan Williams during a public talk with the creator of the TV series *Succession*, which depicts a bunch of awful non-Stoic business types who are completely gripped by every sin going: pride, greed, lust, anger, envy, sloth and gluttony. Rowan said that he saw *Succession* as a moral fable. 'It's fascinating in some ways to depict sin, evil and destructive lives – but the depiction ought to make you realize it would be hell to live like that. And I think *Succession* does that very well.' You could argue that Greek tragedies perform a similar task.

THE AUGUSTINIAN OBJECTION

You've got to love St Augustine of Hippo, the non-stop super-shagger turned saint of fifth-century North Africa. His *Confessions* are a great read, especially the bits about his insatiable courtesan habit. He was very well schooled in the ancient philosophers, and refers frequently to Socrates, Plato, Cicero and Seneca. His objection to Stoicism was briefly this: if it's such a great philosophy, then why did some of its followers commit suicide?

> Happy life, indeed, which seeks the aid of death to end it! If such a life is happy, then I say, live it. If it is happy, let the wise man remain in it; but if these ills drive him out of it, in what sense is it happy? . . . For who is so blind as not to see that if [life] were happy it would not be fled from?

This is what he asks in his book *The City of God*. Christianity, he says, by contrast, offers hope in heaven, and is therefore more positive.

But this objection doesn't really work. Surely you can be both happy in life and decide to end it when you choose? After all, Socrates almost committed suicide, in the sense that he could have escaped his jail if he'd wanted to. A happy suicide is certainly conceivable.

THE NIETZSCHEAN OBJECTION

Do you really want to lead a passionless life?

Nietzsche is slightly Stoic. Triumph and disaster should be treated just the same. He thinks it's almost as stupid to 'consider all forms of distress as objections, as things that need to be done away with', as to complain about the weather. He is a fan of the pre-Socratic philosopher Heraclitus, who taught that the world was in constant flux. He says that one of Zarathustra's doctrines, the 'infinitely repeated circular course of all things', was in Heraclitus, and adds, 'At least the Stoa has traces of it, and the Stoics inherited almost all of their principal notions from Heraclitus.'

But Nietzsche, always at pains to point out that he is the great 'yea-sayer', is hostile towards Stoicism's mission to eradicate passion. 'Is life really so painful and burdensome enough to make it advantageous for us to trade it for a fossilized Stoic way of life?' he asks in *The Gay Science*. He says, simply, that 'passion is better than Stoicism', and that the aim of the Stoics was essentially negative: 'to get as little displeasure as possible out of life'. They're about minimizing trouble, rather than maximizing passion.

Nietzsche has a lovely short peroration on Stoics versus Epicureans. Epicureans, he says, avoid the slings and arrows by retreating to a rural commune, whereas the Stoics aim to put up with it. 'The Stoic trains himself to swallow stones and worms, slivers of glass and scorpions with nausea.' He says that those of us with any foresight and freedom should aim for an Epicurean life, and that those types hate to have their 'irritability' taken away and 'awarded in its place a hard Stoic hedgehog skin'. Spiky, stoney, spiritless: this is how the Stoics seem to

Nietzsche. Maybe it's a shame, for example, that Tolstoy started life as a 'fox', with his Shakespearean ability to inhabit multiple personalities, and ended it as a 'hedgehog', a monomaniac.

This is not a million miles away, in fact, from the Christian view of the Stoics. The former Bishop of Oxford, Robert Harris, thinks that Stoicism is a bit limited and pedestrian by comparison with Christianity. 'OK, so you can bear misfortune with a shrug. Then what? Christianity promises so much more: transcendence, and an afterlife.' The bishop was saying that Christianity is all about the spirit; not about denying it.

Nietzsche may not have been a fan of Christianity, but even he could not deny that the purpose of a cathedral is to lift the soul to the heavens and stimulate out-of-body wonder. Religion offers rock'n'roll. Ecstatic states are experienced in more humble churches. Evangelists start rocking their bodies. Gospel music led to Elvis. You can't imagine the Stoics singing gospel music, and how much joy has that brought the world? 'The Shakers shook and the Quakers quaked,' said Aldous Huxley, approvingly. Elvis renamed the ecstatic shaking 'rock'n'roll'. And, we might add, dervishes whirl. The Stoics showed no interest in rocking, rolling, shaking, singing, whirling or getting high on God's love in some way or another. Boring old fossilized hedgehogs! That, my friends, is the Nietzschean objection.

Leisure

If you want to be happy, do little.
DEMOCRITUS

Make then leisure for thyself for the learning of some good thing more.
MARCUS AURELIUS

Lest we get too idealistic about ancient Athens, let's not forget that for all its artistic and philosophical achievements and general brilliance it was an aristocratic, warlike and slave-owning society where women belonged in the home.

However, a definite upside to this was that the free-wheeling Athenians didn't have a work ethic in today's sense. Jobs and work were not where you found meaning. The hard work like mining was done by slaves who were conscious of their slavery, and no-one claimed, as they do today, that fulfilment can come from a boring, servile job. Meaning, purpose and happiness came not from work – which was sometimes called *ponos* or pain – but from participation in the courts, service in the army, going to drama festivals and drinking wine all night at symposia with your mates.

And from leisure. The Greek word for leisure was *schole*, which meant 'leisure, spare time, ease', and produced words like *skolastikos*, meaning 'being at leisure' or 'devoting all one's leisure to learning'. Our word 'school' is derived from the Latin *scholus*, which itself is derived from *schole*. In the Athenian mind, then, leisure and schooling were closely linked. It seemed desirable to use your leisure time for wandering around in the groves of Academe discussing the *logos*. Socrates had been a sculptor when young, and then a soldier, but in middle and old age he did nothing much beyond wandering around the *agora*, philosophizing. Diogenes clearly never had a job. He was a full-time do-nothing. And later Aristotle recommended that those seeking *eudaimonia* should devote as much time as possible to *schole*.

Otium, like *schole*, had positive connotations. It wasn't the same as laziness. The Latin word *negotium*, not-leisure, meant 'shopping' or 'business', and is where we get our word 'negotiation'. *Otium* was a precious commodity and should be cultivated.

There was a second form of leisure, a less obviously useful one, which the Greeks called *aergia*. This literally meant laziness or sloth, and was named after the goddess of the same name, who was a byword for lounging around on couches, staring into space. The Roman equivalent was *ignavus*. This isn't the sort of leisure that the strict Stoics embraced, though it certainly has its attractions.

Athens' great general Pericles gave a speech praising the Athenian idea of *schole*. Note that he mentions in passing that happiness can be found in interior decoration.

> When our work is over, we are in a position to enjoy all kinds of recreation for our spirits. There are

various kinds of contests and sacrifices regularly held throughout the year; in our own homes we find a beauty and a good taste which delight us every day and which drive away our cares.

We've seen how Zeno, the first Stoic, loved basking in the sun eating figs. His teacher, we remember, had been the Cynic Crates, who didn't seem to do very much in the way of meaningful employment, preferring to indulge in pieces of performance art like throwing bowls of lentils at his students and taking all his clothes off in front of his girlfriend's parents.

At the same time the Stoics were by no means inert. They were far more moderate and worldly than the Cynics. You'll remember that Zeno said that man is 'naturally made for society and action'. Zeno was certainly not in a rush. He saw philosophy as a lifelong object of study: 'Well-being is attained by little and little, and nevertheless it is no little thing itself,' he is supposed to have said.

We could hardly call Cicero a leisure-lover. He was a very busy person: a lawyer, statesman, orator, ruthless courtier and money-maker. However, he did eventually retire from public life following the death of his daughter and the death of Caesar. This is when he wrote the *Tusculan Disputations*, supposedly based on philosophical conversations in his villa. At the end of the fifth essay in the book he praises leisure – using the term *otium*, not *ignavia* – as practically life-saving.

> Let us fix in our recollections the discussions of the last five days. For my part I think too that I shall write them out – for in what way can I better employ my leisure to whatever cause it is due? . . . In doing

> this I cannot readily say how much I shall benefit
> others; at any rate in my cruel sorrows and the various
> troubles which beset me from all sides no other
> consolation could have been found.

Talking philosophy, then, and the act of writing out his conversations, is immensely therapeutic to Cicero. It's consoling.

Seneca wrote a whole essay on the subject, *De Otio*, 'On Leisure', part of which survives. Seneca argued in this essay that retiring to think is a political act in the sense that your contemplation could help the state: you will come up with ideas which might be acted upon. He also says that it is perfectly acceptable to devote yourself to a leisurely, philosophical life from a young age.

> [S]omeone can, perhaps from the first stage of life,
> surrender entirely to the contemplation of truth, to
> seek a coherent intellectual basis [ratio] for living and
> to train himself in private.

This notion of full-time contemplation did indeed come true later on with the invention of the monk and the monastery, itself an evolution of the Platonic Academy.

The difference, Seneca says, between the Epicurean idea of leisure and the Stoic idea of leisure is that with the former it's an end in itself, whereas for the Stoics leisure is desirable because it will produce a social benefit. It's all about leisure with purpose. 'The [Epicurean] makes it his aim in life to seek for leisure; the [Stoic] seeks it only when he has reasons for so doing.' The Stoic philosophers, he says, through their embrace of *otium*, have done more for humanity than the generals of armies.

> What is the wise man's purpose in devoting himself to leisure? He knows that in leisure as well as in action he will accomplish something by which he will be of service to posterity. Our school at any rate declares that Zeno and Chrysippus have done greater things than they would have done had they been in command of armies, or filled high offices, or passed laws.

If you doubt that man was made for contemplation, says Seneca, as an aside, then why does he stand tall and have a bendy neck? He's surely built for star-gazing.

> [Nature] has not only set man erect upon his feet, but also with a view to making it easy for him to watch the heavens, she has raised his head on high and connected it with a pliant neck, in order that he might follow the course of the stars from their rising to their setting, and move his face round with the whole heaven.

A good life embraces both inaction and action: 'Nature... intended me to do both, to practise both contemplation and action: and I do both.' Zeno and Chrysippus, he says, found utility in reflection. 'They found the means of making their retirement more useful to mankind than the perspirings and runnings to and fro of other men.'

Then as now, it seems, people talked about quitting their job in order to become full-time contemplatives. And then as now, people had the idea that they would retire once they'd built up enough cash. Sometimes you hear about young people making a plan to work in the City for ten years and then quit to follow their real dreams, but this rarely actually happens because the young person gets sucked into the money-earning life.

Seneca was similarly impatient with his correspondent Lucilius, who seems to have entertained dreams of quitting his job and becoming a full-time philosopher. Seneca respects this desire because, he says, 'a person of character will not wear himself out with paltry and demeaning labour; he will not engage in business just for the sake of being busy.' But Lucilius is dilly-dallying because he likes the money and the servants.

> It is easy to escape from your job, dear Lucilius, if you have no regard for the rewards of the job. It is the rewards that hinder us and keep us at it . . . Shall my sedan chair be unattended?

If Lucilius is delaying because he's worrying about 'how large your retirement income will be then you will never find release. As long as you hang on to the suitcase, you cannot swim to safety.'

If you want more leisure, Seneca is saying, then take it now. Don't procrastinate for financial reasons.

Marcus Aurelius echoes Seneca's insistence that just 'being busy' is ridiculous. Purposeless perspiring should be avoided, he says. Doing as little as possible is not laziness, it's efficiency. And a ruthless cutting out of superfluous activity will lead to sweet *otium*.

> Most of what we say and do is unnecessary: remove the superfluity, and you will have more time and less bother. So in every case one should prompt oneself: 'Is this, or is it not, something necessary?' And the removal of the unnecessary should apply not only

to actions but to thoughts also: then no redundant actions either will follow.

What a contrast with the modern idea that busy is good. Marcus Aurelius would have argued that busy is stupid. Being super-busy just means you're disorganized and have no idea how to use your time well.

Epictetus says that the true Cynic, like an Indian *saddhu* or Buddhist monk today, would never marry and have children, because domestic life would interfere with his duty to serve God and mankind. In making this argument, Epictetus gives us a tantalizing glimpse of family life in the ancient world, when, it appears, young Dads were more hands-on than we might have imagined.

> He must get a kettle to heat water for the baby, for washing it in a bathtub; wool for his wife when she has had a child, oil, a cot, a cup – the vessels get more and more numerous . . . Where is the man who is tied down to the duties of everyday life going to find leisure? . . . Doesn't he have to get little cloaks for the children? Doesn't he have to send them off to the schoolteacher with their little note tablets and writing implements?

And make packed lunches for them? And help them with their homework? Truly, the renunciate must cast off these distractions.

Of course the Cynic, *saddhu* or monkish path is unrealistic for most of us. But we can all make time for *schole*. It's free. Like modern people, the Romans were continually dashing off to some holiday resort like Baiae or

Lanuvium. Why couldn't they just stay at home, asked Marcus Aurelius, and find peace within?

> Men seek out retreats for themselves in the country, by the seaside, in the mountains . . . but all this is unphilosophical to the last degree, when you can at a moment's notice retire into yourself.

You'll save a lot of cash that way too.

So our conclusion here is: be scholarly, be leisurely. And now let's look at what Stoics had to say about good cheer and a sunny disposition.

17

Cheerfulness

> EDWARDS. *'You are a philosopher, Dr Johnson.
> I have tried too in my time to be a philosopher; but,
> I don't know how, cheerfulness was always breaking in.'*
> – *Mr Burke, Sir Joshua Reynolds, Mr Courtenay,
> Mr Malone and, indeed, all the eminent men to whom
> I have mentioned this, have thought it an exquisite
> trait of character. The truth is, that philosophy, like
> religion, is too generally supposed to be hard and severe,
> at least so grave as to exclude all gaiety.'*
> BOSWELL'S *LIFE OF SAMUEL JOHNSON*

One of Dickens' most lovable characters must be the ever-cheerful Mark Tapley in *Martin Chuzzlewit*. Like Cat Stevens in 'Moonshadow', he takes looking on the bright side to new and absurd heights. He actively dislikes so-called 'good' things happening as they make it too easy to be jolly. When he leaves his comfy job at the Blue Dragon he tells landlady Mrs Lupin, 'I'm always a-thinking that with my good health and spirits it would be more creditable in me to be jolly where there's things a-going on to make one dismal.' He tells Martin that he'd relish a bad employer.

'An envious family or a quarrelsome family, or a malicious family, or even a good out-and-out mean family, would open a field of action as I might do something in.'

Mark Tapley remains jolly in the midst of the malaria-soaked misery he and Martin endure after falling victim to a land sale scam in America. 'Things is looking about as bad as they can look, young man,' he says to himself when they are at their lowest ebb.

> You'll not have such another opportunity for showing your jolly disposition, my fine fellow, as long as you live. And therefore, Tapley, Now's your time to come out strong; or Never!

I'd say that Mark Tapley is a good candidate to be celebrated as an ideal Stoic wise man.

Dickens contrasts Mark Tapley with the miserable, scrounging, anti-Stoic Chevy Slyme, who, when caught out not paying his bill at the Blue Dragon, whinges,

> I am the wretchedest creature on record. Society is in a conspiracy against me. I'm the most literary man alive. I'm full of scholarship. I'm full of genius; I'm full of information; I'm full of novel views on every subject; yet look at my condition! I'm at this moment obliged to two strangers for a tavern bill!

We've all met such types. Some people appear to have all the external benefits of riches, friends and leisure, and are thoroughly miserable. Others, meanwhile, remain cheerful even when the circs are tricky.

So Dr Johnson's friend, quoted above, is quite wrong when he says that philosophy (by which he may well mean

Stoicism) excludes all gaiety. When we survey the Stoic writings we find much severity, to be sure, but there's also an insistence on positive thinking and a shiny glow.

The Greeks would have said that Mark Tapley was overflowing with *euthymia* or good cheer. He uses the power of his mind to stay cheerful. In *The Anatomy of Melancholy*, the great seventeenth-century self-help manual, Robert Burton quotes Seneca as saying,

> I have seen men miserably dejected in a pleasant village, and some again well occupied and at good ease in a solitary desert; 'tis the mind, not the place, causeth tranquillity, and gives good content.

Cheerfulness, goes the Stoic line, is a result of mental attitude, not of external circumstances.

The early Stoics didn't sound like a barrel of laughs, though, and possibly were a little 'hard and severe', in the words of Dr Johnson's friend Edwards. Zeno was called 'niggardly of countenance', and Chrysippus was accused of being stern and arrogant (though he did die laughing at his own feeble joke concerning asses and figs). There's not much mention of cheerfulness in Cicero, perhaps because he loved the severe Cato.

However, cheerfulness was and is, I'd argue, a Stoic virtue. After all, Xanthippe had praised her husband Socrates for always wearing the same cheery expression, whether leaving the house in the morning or returning at night (though that didn't stop her from pouring the chamber pot over his head).

Marcus Aurelius is certainly a fan of a cheery temperament. He praises his friend Maximus for his 'cheerfulness in sickness as well as in all other circumstances'. The word

Marcus uses here is *euthumon*. He also praises his father for being always *phaidros*, meaning 'radiant with joy', and uses the same word when he encourages his readers to be *phaidros*, i.e. sunny of disposition, in Book III. In Book X he argues that good cheer follows from a Stoic temperament. 'He who follows Reason [*logos*] in everything shall be leisurely without being lethargic and cheerful [*phaidron*] as well as composed.'

In similar fashion Epictetus, quoting Musonius Rufus, reckons that all the virtues will come in the wake of 'the power to make use of external impressions'. Once you can do this, he says, then four desirable states of being follow, of which 'cheerfulness' is third in the list: 'Freedom, serenity, cheerfulness, steadfastness'.

The Greek words here are: *eleutheria, euroia, euthumia* and *enstatheia*. Quite a nice bunch of qualities to aim for. And as with any skill, you have to practise. Diogenes argued that more people would be happy if they spent more time practising to be happy. Imagine doing an hour a day's cheerfulness practice. In time you might get quite good at it.

Nietzsche, though anti-Stoic, as we have seen, forced himself to be cheerful out of philosophical duty. In *Human, All Too Human* he says,

> I learned the art of presenting myself as if I was cheerful, objective, inquisitive . . . all of this ultimately resulted in a great spiritual strengthening, an increasing pleasure and abundance of health. Life itself rewards us for stubborn will to life, for a long war such as I waged at that time against the pessimism of weariness with life.

Pretend to be cheerful and you will become cheerful. Wage war against pessimism. Serious and severe books, too, says Nietzsche, can bring cheer in their wake.

> [A] book appearing to be cold and sober can, when seen with the right eyes, seem to be played upon by the sunshine of spiritual cheerfulness [*geistigen Heiterkeit*] and a true source of comfort for the soul.

Nietzsche finds cheerfulness in acceptance and a refusal to be negative. He says he loves fate whatever it throws at him. He aspired not merely to withstand misfortune with equanimity, but to embrace it fervently.

> Not merely bear what is necessary, still less conceal it . . . but love it . . . *Amor fati*: let that be my love henceforth! I do not want to wage war against what is ugly. I do not want to accuse; I do not even want to accuse those who accuse. Looking away shall be my only negation. And all in all and on the whole: some day I wish to be only a Yes-sayer.

Saying yes to life means saying yes to death, the subject of our next chapter.

18

Death

No wailing can recall the dead.
SENECA, *AD MARCIAM DE CONSOLATIONE*

There is nothing more certain than the fact that death awaits every one of us. Yet we all live as if it will never happen.
TOLSTOY

Mary Shelley was in Venice with her young husband when her three-year-old daughter Clara died. The body was buried on the beach at the Lido. This was the second child the couple had lost. It was September; the year was 1818; Mary was 20 years old and in January had published her first novel, *Frankenstein*. She wrote to her father, the radical philosopher William Godwin, telling him how horribly depressed she was. He replied to her in decidedly Stoic fashion. He told her – well, not exactly to just 'cheer up' – but that she had a moral responsibility to move on.

> What is it you want that you have not? You have the husband of your choice, to whom you seem to

be unalterably attached, a man of high intellectual endowments . . . You have all the goods of fortune, all the means of being useful to others, & shining in your proper sphere. But you have lost a child: & all the rest of the world, all that is beautiful, & all that has a claim upon your kindness, is nothing, because a child of three years old is dead!

Er, possibly a bit harsh, there, Dad. He goes on to implore his daughter not to abandon herself to grief – not her, the brilliant Mary! – who has so much to give to the world. Godwin was motivated by love, says Mary's biographer Miranda Seymour. He was worried that his melancholic daughter might give up completely and take her own life. '[D]o not put the miserable delusion on yourself, to think there is something fine, & beautiful, & delicate, in giving yourself up, & agreeing to be nothing.'

I'm not sure whether Mary found these words consoling. Today they'd certainly be seen as a bit cold and unfeeling, even if intended to fortify. But they were in a tradition of Stoic reflections on death. The letter of consolation was a literary form. Cicero had written a *consolatio* to himself after losing his daughter Tullia (though this has not survived), and Seneca wrote three consolations, the *Ad Marciam*, the *Ad Polybium* and the *Ad Helvium*.

Seneca's friend Marcia, a Roman aristocrat, had lost a son, Metilius, and simply could not stop grieving. Even time, Seneca says, could not heal the wound. In *Ad Marciam* he writes, with admirable sympathy, 'Three whole years have now passed, and yet the first violence of your sorrow remains unabated. Your grief is renewed and grows stronger every day.'

Then as now, friends were not sure how to behave towards the bereaved parent. 'None of them know how to conduct themselves; whether they should mention [your dead son] or not.' It is surely better to talk about your son, he says, and celebrate his achievements, rather than make his name unmentionable and retreat into nothingness. Don't agree to be nothing.

The only solution to such a deep-seated grief, Seneca says, is to use violent means to cauterize it. The argument he sets out sounds distinctly Mark Tapley-esque.

> It is no great thing to show oneself brave in the midst of prosperity, when life glides on in a tranquil course; a quiet sea and a favouring wind do not show the skill of a pilot either – some hardship must be encountered that will test his soul.

But surely it's natural to grieve, he imagines Marcia objecting. Yes, but only temporarily. Look at the cows. They grieve for two days then move on. Birds, he says, 'rage against their empty nests, yet in a trice become quiet and resume their ordinary flight'. He holds up the example of Caesar, who was conquering Britain when he heard that his daughter had died. 'Within three days he returned to his duties as general, and conquered his grief as quickly as he was wont to conquer everything else.' OK, maybe a psychopathic, all-conquering tyrant is not a great example. But in our own time we might admire people like Nick Cave, who have been bereaved of their own children but have continued to embrace life, and even become happy again.

And we all make the mistake, Seneca says, of failing to prepare ourselves for misfortune. We wander about with the delusion that bad things only happen to other people, despite the fact that we see friends losing their children, or their money, and we go to plenty of funerals. 'We never anticipate any evil before it arrives, and imagine that we ourselves are exempt.' But, he insists, 'that man lost his children. You may also lose yours.'

Death, Seneca goes on to say, comes to us all. 'Your son is dead; that is, he has finished his course and reached the goal towards which all those whom you count more fortunate than your child are now hastening.' He cites the inscription at Delphi, 'Know thyself' [which he translates as *nosce te*], and says that it refers to man's frailty: 'a fabric of weak and unstable elements'. It's the ancient equivalent of the 1980s bumper sticker, 'Life's a bitch and then you die.'

In what is a stirring and at times beautiful essay, which I'm going to send to my bereaved friends, Seneca goes on to describe the beauty of the world in the fashion of a Romantic poet or, again, Cat Stevens. He eulogizes the mountains and islands and lakes, all of God's creation. 'And what of the gleaming of precious stones and jewels?' he rhapsodizes (I think he may have pastiched this from a bit in the *Phaedo* dialogue where Socrates looks down at the earth from above).

And like Socrates, Seneca said that death was not to be feared. Talk of Hades and everlasting torments was nonsense.

> Reflect that there are no ills to be suffered after death, that the reports that make the Lower World terrible to us are mere tales, that no darkness is in store for the dead, no prison, no blazing streams of fire, no Lethe, that no judgement seats are there, nor culprits . . .
> All these things are the fancies of the poets who have harrowed us with groundless terrors.

He then repeats a familiar consolation: 'Death is a release from all suffering.' It's a return to our pre-natal state and nothing to be feared. After all, Socrates had said that those who live a philosophical life welcome death, look forward to it. His soul will be freed, he says in the *Phaedo*, from the shackles of the body. Socrates actively looks forward to his death. He will be pure soul once again, with no cumbersome body to nag at him with its strange demands.

Epictetus repeated that the way to prepare for death is to live well and virtuously. The best thing would be to die while behaving in exemplary Stoic fashion, as did Socrates.

> I would like it if death overtook me while I was occupied by nothing but my own moral purpose, trying to make it tranquil, unhampered, unconstrained, free.

He has a witty euphemism for death, and you can imagine his young students chuckling as he declaims it: 'It is now time for the material of which you are constituted to be restored to those elements from which it came.'

Marcus Aurelius says something similar. We are dust and to dust we return: 'Fail not to note how short-lived are all mortal things, and how paltry – yesterday a little mucus, tomorrow a mummy or burnt ash.' A longer life, says Marcus, is not a better life. Long and short are the same.

> Small, in any point of view, is the difference in length . . . count it then of no consequence. For look at the yawning gulf of time behind you, and at the infinity of time to come.

He admits that he doesn't know what death is. 'Whether it is a dispersion, or a resolution into atoms, or annihilation, it is either extinction or change.' If it's extinction, then we will have nothing to worry about, as we'll be blissfully unaware.

My friend Charles Handy, a great writer and so-called 'management guru', and something of a philosopher, lived till he was 92. Handy was famous for books like *The Empty Raincoat* and *Gods of Management*, which argued that we all need a greater purpose than just getting and spending and climbing up the ladder. Towards the end he loved reading Stoic philosophy. What he took from Epictetus and the others is that there is a natural order of things, and that death, obviously, is a part of that order. 'I am sorry', he wrote in the *Idler*,

> you too will die, but you will live on processed into the memory of things by the people who knew you and loved you. That is your after life, that's your new life, that's the end of your proper life. That is what you are there for, part of the natural order of things.

Handy tells the story of his Stoic housekeeper, whose response to pretty much any major event was, 'Never mind!' When Handy spilled a glass of wine she'd say, 'Never mind!' When he announced with some pride that he'd been given a job which involved moving to Windsor Castle, where he'd be working with Prince Philip: 'Never mind!'

It was the same, Handy said, when he thought he was dying.

> I was taken aback yesterday morning when I woke up, feeling pretty weak I must say, and pretty sure that I had a heart attack coming on, which I'd been warned

> would happen. So when she said to me in a sprightly way, 'How are you this morning?' I said, 'I think it's the day I'm going to die.' And she said, 'Never mind!'

This did not please Handy. 'At first I was furious. I had just made the most important statement of my life and she had dismissed it as inconsequential.' But on further reflection he realized the wisdom behind this comment. The housekeeper was wisely indifferent to external events, whether a spillage, a promotion or death.

> Well, perhaps she's right, perhaps it is part of the great scheme of things, like the walnut tree I grew 50 years ago, which grew and flourished and dropped its nuts all over the floor, and is now wilting and fading and weakening, just like me, and soon will go.

Nevermind was of course the title of Nirvana's brilliant album of 1991. At the time it was assumed that Kurt Cobain was making some sort of comment on the degenerate apathy of the slacker generation. But maybe we could reinterpret it as a sign of the band's adherence to the Stoic creed. Cobain famously committed suicide – and suicide was by no means forbidden by the Stoics. It was admired. Cato the Younger (grandson of Cato the Elder) had disembowelled himself when he saw that the Republic had fallen.

As for the manner of death of our seven Stoics, they left their bodies in very different ways. Zeno died of old age, when possibly 98 or more. Says Diogenes Laertius:

> The manner of his death was as follows. As he was leaving the school he tripped and fell, breaking a toe.

> Striking the ground with his fist, he quoted the line from the *Niobe*: 'I come, I come, why dost thou call me for?' and died on the spot through holding his breath.

Chrysippus, as we've heard, was supposed to have died laughing at his own joke. Cicero's death was violent. At 63 he was assassinated in his villa by Marc Antony's soldiers. Of Musonius Rufus's manner of death we know nothing. He'd been exiled a couple of times (the emperor was worried that philosophers would inspire tyrannicide), but returned to Rome. He was born in something like 30 AD and died in 102 AD so would have been 72 or thereabouts when he died.

Seneca had hoped to die with the same sort of fortitude and cheerfulness as his hero, Socrates, but it all went a bit pear-shaped. He'd been convicted of involvement in a plot to kill Nero. Nero then ordered him to commit suicide. Seneca and his wife Paulina apparently both cut the veins of their wrists. Paulina was rescued by soldiers, who bound her wrists and survived.

And Seneca didn't die either. His biographer Emily Wilson tells us that he was too old and skinny for the blood to flow out. So he made another cut, this time behind his knees, but that didn't work either. So he called for hemlock, which he'd stored away for this purpose, and took it, but still no luck. He was annoyingly alive.

Finally, says Wilson,

> He stepped into a dish of hot water, spattering the poor slaves standing nearby: this spill was, he said, a libation to Jupiter the Liberator. Finally he had his slaves lift him into a hot bath, and he suffocated in the steam. They cremated him immediately, according to his wish.

He was 69.

Blimey. What a palaver.

Epictetus was supposed to have been 85 when he died. Of his manner of death we know nothing. As for Marcus Aurelius, no-one is entirely sure how he croaked. The movie *Gladiator* accuses his evil son Commodus of doing the deed, but equally he may have died of illness. He was only 58. So if you want long life – and you may not – it would seem wiser to be a full-time philosopher like Zeno or Epictetus rather than attempt to combine the philosophical life with a life of action, like Cicero, Seneca and Marcus. The less active arguably live longer.

All our seven Stoics have left a lingering and wonderful legacy, millennia after they died. They can all be read today for pleasure and instruction and inspiration. Thanks to their own writings or the notes of their enraptured students, we can talk to them now. And certainly Cicero, Seneca and Marcus Aurelius, being ambitious coves, were writing in the hope of being read by later generations. They were very conscious of leaving a legacy, not just a pile of cash.

So now let's look at the legacy of the Stoics. It's not always good. The go-getting bros of the American Empire in particular have distorted their teachings into a sort of patriarchal, competitive, amoral 'beat the other guy' ethic.

19

Legacy

If you want to become successful, masculine, if you want to make a lot of money, if you want to date and sleep with a lot of girls . . . be Stoic.
YOUTUBE VIDEO (WE WILL
NOT DIGNIFY THE PRESENTER
WITH HIS NAME)

A terrible injustice has been done to the Seven Stoics. Two thousand years after the death of Marcus Aurelius, the buff, greedy, combative leaders of the so-called 'manosphere' – people like Andrew Tate, Joe Rogan and Tim Ferriss – have claimed to inherit the Stoic legacy. But it's nonsense. As we've seen, the basis of Stoicism is to be entirely indifferent to the external things that most people value – money, fame, honour and so on. Instead you should cultivate your inner daimon, your peaceful essence. These charlatans promise their young, insecure male followers money, sex and power and claim that 'being Stoic' will get you these external things. Which is pretty much the exact opposite of what Stoicism really means. Stoics are against greed and lust, and they counsel against depending on external things for one's happiness.

The boy-men of the manosphere – which should be called the childosphere, as these idiots still cherish an adolescent fantasy of what it means to be a man – find the tough, Roman elements of the Stoic philosophy appealing. That one of the Seven Stoics was an emperor gives them a way in. 'You're getting the direct thoughts of the man who ruled Rome,' as Joe Rogan enthused when he boasted about reading the *Meditations* (though he then confessed it was an audiobook).

Earlier and more benign versions of bro culture were influenced by the Stoics. They've been well used in self-help books, and the inventor of that genre, Samuel Smiles, author of the severe Victorian pull-yourself-up-by-your-own-bootstraps manual for ambitious young men, *Self-Help*, mentions both Cicero and Seneca as role models. A 1958 lecture by Isiah Berlin, 'Two Concepts of Liberty', cited the Stoics and their idea of 'self-mastery', which Berlin compared to his second type of freedom, positive freedom.

An oft-mentioned Stoic story is the tale of Admiral Stockdale. In his book and lectures he talks about how clinging on to Stoic principles of remaining happy within even under torture sustained him for a seven-year stint as a prisoner of war in Vietnam. He was tortured frequently and spent two years in leg irons. His example has inspired books like *Stoic Wisdom: Ancient Lessons in Modern Resilience* by Nancy Sherman, which again repackages Stoicism as a survival technique for tough guys and ignores its religious and mystical dimensions.

Another oft-cited example of Stoics in literature is the great Tom Wolfe's *A Man in Full*. When the hero Charlie Croker loses his fortune, his carer Conrad Hemsley introduces the 60-year-old to Epictetus.

'What does Epictetus have to say about bankruptcy? – or is that something too mundane for a philosopher to think about?'

'Not too mundane for Epictetus, Mr Croker. One place he says, "You are all nervous and you can't sleep at night for fear you're going to run out of money. You say, 'How will I even get enough to eat?' But what you are really afraid of is not starvation but the prospect of not having a cook or somebody to wait on you at the dinner table or somebody to take care of your clothes and your shoes and the laundry and make up the beds and clean up the house. In other words, you're afraid you may no longer be able to lead the life of an invalid."'

A key Stoic legacy is cognitive behavioural therapy or CBT. This is a very successful and popular form of therapy that aims to teach people how to control their reactions to external events. Aaron Beck, its bow-tied founder, was a fan of the Stoics. He died in 2021 aged 100. In 2007 he told the philosopher Jules Evans (who in 2012 wrote a very good book on Stoicism called *Life and Other Dangerous Situations*) that he was 'influenced by the Stoic philosophers who stated that it was a meaning of events rather than the events themselves that affected people'. In other words, how we react to situations is up to us.

And philosophers are fascinated by the fact that ideas explored 2,500 years ago can have such practical effects today. 'CBT is now the most scientifically credible and popular form of therapy for many emotional disorders,' Jules Evans wrote.

> To my mind it is fascinating that CBT has built up an evidence base to show that the Stoics' ideas and

techniques for transforming the emotions
genuinely work. It is extraordinary that ideas
about the emotions conceived two millennia ago
should still be our best guide for healing
the emotions today.

Unlike Stoicism, though, CBT is secular and unpolitical. There is no mention in its tenets of either God or Providence or the evils of governments and tyrants. CBT removes the spiritual component of Stoicism and renders it wholly practical, a means of coping in the material world.

You could also argue that, like other forms of therapy, CBT puts a heavy burden on the individual and ignores injustice. It encourages you to accept the world as it is rather than try to change it by, for example, protesting. If the Suffragettes had been prescribed CBT, might they have simply accepted that they couldn't vote? And some critics, including my mate Mark Vernon, an author and psychotherapist, reckon its benefits can be short-lived. But many swear by it, and it's certainly a successful offshoot of Stoicism.

The most enduring legacy of Stoicism, though, is not bro-culture or CBT. It's peace and love. Christianity, as we've seen, at least for St Paul, was deeply influenced by Stoic ideas of commanding the passions, of resisting the demons. The passions of the Stoics evolved into the seven deadly sins of the early Christians. And though the Greeks and Romans were slave-owning societies, you can see, at least in Seneca, some of the compassion for fellow men that would become a hallmark of Christianity. He writes with humanity in one of the letters to Lucilius of his horror at how slaves are treated.

> I am pleased to learn from those who have been with you that you live on familiar terms with your slaves. This is becoming in a person of your sense and education.
>
> 'They are slaves.' No, they are human beings.
>   'They are slaves.' No, they are housemates.
>   'They are slaves.' No, they are low-born friends.

He then attacks people who 'think it is beneath them to share a meal with their slaves'. He is appalled by men who sexually abuse their boy-slaves: 'He is on duty all night: his first shift is devoted to his master's drinking, his second to his lust.' And anyway, fortune could reverse your roles, he says. 'It is possible you will see him a free man, and that he will see you enslaved.'

The Christians went much further: they later attempted to outlaw slavery, and the medieval city states wrote anti-slavery statements into their constitutions. Slavery tragically came back after the Renaissance, as we know, when so-called Christians shipped men and women from Africa to work in hellish sugar and tobacco plantations to enable English gentlemen to buy mansions in Wiltshire, go hunting and give their daughters lessons on the spinet. Nowadays aspiring English gentlemen who crave an Eton education for their sons and a modest estate work as lawyers and fixers for Russian oil oligarchs and Saudi princes.

The Stoic idea of the *logos* has centre stage in the Bible, where it's used in the prologue to St John's Gospel. It's generally translated as 'the Word'. We looked at this earlier. We've also seen the Stoic legacy in St Augustine, who was well read in the ancients. St Paul debated with the Stoics and Epicureans at the Areopagus. He disagreed with them because they appeared to worship multiple gods, whereas he said there was just one, and that he's inside all of us.

We could argue that the Christian martyrs behaved in Stoic fashion. They willingly and even cheerfully allowed their bodies to be torn apart in various gruesome ways. Their inner happiness could not be affected by things that were done to the body, which reminds us of the Stoic notion of endurance under torture.

And there's Gandhi. The academic Richard Sorabji has written a book called *Gandhi and the Stoics*, which draws a line between Stoic ideas of indifference and Hindu ideas of non-attachment. He says he sees parallels between the early Christians and their seven deadly sins, and Gandhi's attempts to be celibate. Sorabji says that both the Stoics and Gandhi believed in family love, but also that love should be detached. This will mean that we do not become completely consumed with self-pity when a loved one dies.

As far as non-violence and turning the other cheek go, well, that was the bit of the Sermon on the Mount that captivated Tolstoy, and it was Tolstoy who inspired Gandhi to take up non-violence as a means of achieving independence for India. In 1884 Tolstoy wrote in his diary, 'I have to create a circle of reading for myself: Epictetus, Marcus Aurelius, Lao-Tzu, Buddha, Pascal, the New Testament. This is also necessary for all people.' Note that the first two sages he mentions are both Stoics (this project turned into a book called *A Calendar of Wisdom*). He later corresponded with Gandhi. (You can read the letters for free online.) So while Gandhi may not have read the Stoics, he certainly read and was inspired by people who had read them. It's not too fanciful to say: no Stoics, no Indian independence.

There are innumerable Stoic-lovers in literature. Dante places Cato in Purgatory and Seneca in Limbo. These are signs that he approved of them; otherwise they would have gone to hell. In Chaucer's *The Tale of Melibee*, a wealthy merchant goes for a walk in the country, leaving his wife and daughter alone in his house. While he's out, some evil men break in and beat up the wife and leave the daughter with five mortal wounds. This leads to a long discussion between man and wife on how to deal with pain, during which Seneca is cited no less than 17 times.

> Seneca says: 'The wise man shall not take too great discomfort for the death of his children, but, certainly, he should suffer it in patience.'

We see the Stoic creed, too, in Baloo's song in the Disney film of *The Jungle Book*, 'The Bare Necessities'. If only you could concentrate on the important things, says Baloo, you would 'forget about your worries and your strife'. And here we can draw a line back to Kipling who memorably advised,

> If you can meet with triumph and disaster
> And treat those two impostors just the same

… then you'll be a man, my son!

A further, perhaps minor, legacy is the Stoic look. Beard, sandals, simple cloak, stick, lentil-eating, a love of figs. It's a look that's been stolen again and again by monks, friars, hippies and now even ayahuasca-taking billionaire's sons on Ibiza with their man-buns and flip-flops.

What, then, has the Stoic creed offered its fans whether Christians, Romantic poets, Tolstoy, or punks – or since it was founded in ancient Athens? If one word sums it up, it's 'liberation'. Stoicism gives you the freedom to act and react as you choose. No other man can get inside my head and force me what to think. Stoics are anti-tyrannical, anarchistic; they believe in the authority of the self. They believe in frugality as a path to freedom. They believe in questioning the authorities, for not to do so is to be slave-like. Remember how Epictetus banishes his pupils by calling them 'slave'? What he means is they have not thought for themselves. They are trapped in ready-made ideologies. They must, as William Blake suggested, cast off the mind-forg'd manacles and move forward to freedom.

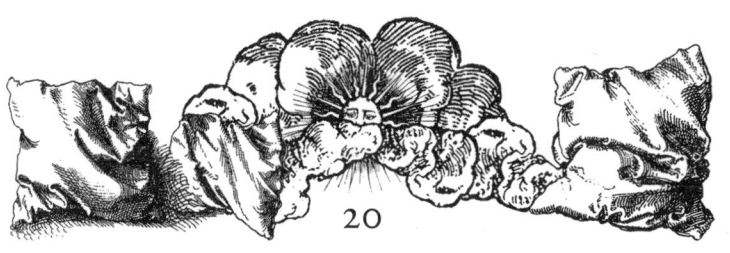

Conclusion

*Everything that can make us better and happier
God has placed directly in front of us,
or at least very close to us.*

SENECA

Some readers may be wondering, what about the author of this book? Is he a Stoic? Does he practise what he appears to have been preaching? The simple answer would be no.

That's not because it doesn't work. I admit that reading a good dose of Seneca, Epictetus or Cicero each day while researching this book did calm me down somewhat. It made me happier. Tolstoy is right: commune with the wise and be happy.

For one thing, I think the doctrine of indifference is very powerful and very useful. Just saying the words, 'I remain supremely indifferent', helps you to become genuinely indifferent to minor and even major annoyances, and see them all as part of the mysterious plan. It's true that you can train your mind to get stronger. You start with not getting annoyed when a cup breaks. And you end by remaining calm and even happy if your child dies.

I love the Stoics' sense of fate and destiny, and their idea of being in harmony with your inner 'daimon' or conscience. I aspire to their exalted level of detachment. And I agree with them that simply indulging every bad emotion that invades us is weak-willed. If you do that, you're just a ball in a pinball machine, being flipped around by external forces. I love their rejection of fame, glory, wealth and the satisfaction of lust as the aims of life. I love their hints of compassion.

But. I have two main objections. One is that the wise Stoic would be insufferably smug.

Another is this. It does not allow for Dionysian revelry. Just the other day, my friend M. and I spent the day at a meeting of the Lute Society. We very much enjoyed the polite Renaissance and baroque music. However, as the concert finished we were joined by three other friends, my mate M.'s wife and another couple. We went for a drink at the Cheshire Cheese in Fleet Street, but got stuck with a stranger who sat at our table (we wanted to chat to each other). As a ruse to get rid of her, M. made a show of booking a session at a karaoke bar on his phone. We all stood up and the stranger left. We waited for her to leave the room and then we sat down again. 'That worked!' said M. However, he really had booked a karaoke session. We groaned but went along with it.

Then once we got to the karaoke bar one of our party brought out some gummies and magic mushroom drops. We drank a couple of margaritas. Having initially been a bit buttoned-up, we all let go and started singing and dancing to Abba, Oasis and Bob Dylan with abandon. When our time was up we went into the main bar, where we carried on dancing. (We're all in our late fifties, I should add, with grown-up children). I even got on the ground

CONCLUSION

and spun around in an attempt at break dancing. It was fantastic fun, and on the way home on the Underground I thought, I don't want to be a Stoic. Stoics (if indeed there are any genuine Stoics in the world, which I doubt) are too self-controlled, too puritanical. They don't allow for freaking out, for going mental, for losing the self, for ecstatic release, for leaping about. I found myself agreeing with Nietzsche: there's something a bit fossilized about them.

Maybe the Stoics are happy. Robert Burton said that melancholy attacks everybody except for fools and Stoics. Those stone-like Stoics are, he writes, 'never troubled by any kind of passion, but without blood or feeling; they are almost like the gods'. Human beings are full of blood and passion, and though we'd like to be godlike, it won't happen to most of us.

That's not to say that I reject the Stoic teachers. Far from it. I love them, I love studying them and would recommend all seven of them to everyone. I'd also advise you not to bother with books about the Stoics (apart from this one, of course), but to go back to the actual texts themselves. They're easily available in cheap editions, Penguin Classics, World's Classics or Everyman's. Just a few lines before you go to bed are truly nourishing to the spirit, and while you may never become wise, you can, at least very slowly, move towards wisdom.

Bibliography and Further Reading

Augustine, St, *Confessions*, ed, Temple Scott with introduction by Alice Meynell, Grant Richards, 1904
Marcus Aurelius, trs. C. R. Haines, Harvard, 1930
Marcus Aurelius, *Meditations*, trs. Maxwell Staniforth, Penguin, 1964
Bakewell, Sarah, *How to Live: A Life of Montaigne in one question and twenty attempts at an answer*, Vintage, 2011
Burton, Robert, *The Anatomy of Melancholy*, NYRB, 2001
Cicero, *On the Orator, On Fate, Stoic Paradoxes, The Divisions of Oratory*, trs. H. Rackham, Harvard, 1942
—*Tusculan Disputations*, trs. J. E. King, Harvard, 1945
Desmond, William, *Cynics*, Acumen, 2008
Dickens, Charles, *Martin Chuzzlewit*, Everyman's Library, 1994
Diogenes Laertius, *Books 1–5*, trs. R. D. Hicks, Harvard, 1972
—*Books 6–10*, trs. R. D. Hicks, Harvard, 1972
Epictetus, *Discourses, Books 1–2*, trs. W. A. Oldfather, Harvard, 1925
—*Discourses, Books 3–4, Fragments, The Encheiridion*, Harvard, 1928
—*Discourses, Fragments, Handbook*, trs. Robin Hard with introduction and notes by Christopher Gill, Oxford World's Classics, 2014
John, Elton, *Me*, Macmillan, 2019
Lane, Melissa, *Greek and Roman Political Ideas*, Pelican, 2014

Long, A. A. and Sedley, D. N., *The Hellenistic Philosophers I: Translations of the Principal Sources, With Philosophical Commentary*, Cambridge, 1987

Montaigne, *Essays and Letters, Books 1–5*, ed. William Hazlitt, Navarre Society, 1923

Musonius Rufus, *That One Should Disdain Hardships: The Teachings of a Roman Stoic*, trs. Cora E. Lutz, introduction by Gretchen Reydams-Schils, Yale, 2020

Nietzsche, Friedrich, *The Gay Science*, trs. Walter Kaufmann, Vintage, 1974

—*On the Geneaology of Morals*, trs. Walter Kaufmann, Vintage, 1969

—*Human, All Too Human*, trs. Marion Faber, Penguin, 2004

The Philokalia: Volume One, trs. and ed. G. E. H. Palmer, Philip Sherrard and Kalliston Ware, Faber and Faber, 1979

Pigliucci, Massimo, *How to Be a Stoic: Using Ancient Philosophy to Live a Modern Life*, Penguin, 2017

Seneca, *Moral Essays 1*, trs. John W. Basore, Harvard, 1928

—*Moral Essays 2*, trs. John W. Basore, Harvard, 1928

—*Letters on Ethics*, trs. Margaret Craver and A. A. Long, Chicago, 2017

Seymour, Miranda, *Mary Shelley*, Simon and Schuster, 2000

Sherman, Nancy, *Stoic Wisdom: Ancient Lessons for Modern Resilience*, Oxford, 2021

Sorabji, Richard, *Gandhi and the Stoics: Modern Experiments in Ancient Values*, Oxford, 2016

Taylor, John, *Greek to GCSE 1*, Bloomsbury, 2016

Tolstoy, Leo, *A Calendar of Wisdom*, trs. Roger Cockrell, Alma, 2015

Williams, Rowan, *Passions of the Soul*, Bloomsbury Continuum, 2024

Wilson, Emily, *Seneca: A Life*, Allen Lane, 2014

Glossary of Greek Terms

adiaphora, indifferents, free from differences

anaideia, shamelessness, like a dog

apatheia, freedom from passion or emotion

arche, the beginning

argos, lazy

arete, virtue

ataraxia, inner tranquillity

athaumastia, freedom from surprise or wonder

autarkia, 'rule over oneself' or self-sufficiency, the state of needing nothing external

autopragia, the power of independent action

chreiai, proverbs, stories

demos, the people

doulos, slave

diatribe, discourse, philosophical conversation, originally 'a means of passing the time'

ekklesia, assembly (from which we get ecclesiastical)

eleutheria, freedom

GLOSSARY OF GREEK TERMS

eros, passionate love

eudaimonia, happiness, literally 'good demon-ness'

eudoxia, good name, reputation

euroia, serenity

euthumia, cheerfulness

kosmopolites, citizen of the universe or cosmos

kratos, power

logikos, logic

logos, divine reason, the way

paideuthentas, education

paradoxa, against received wisdom

parrhesia, freedom of speech, invented by Diogenes, admired by Foucault

pathos, emotion

phaidros, radiant with joy

phantasia, impression

philia, friendship, love

politeia, the republic, the citizenry, the commonwealth

ponos, both 'work' and 'pain'

pronoia, foreknowledge

psyche, soul

pythos, storage jar, the sort of earthenware container in which Diogenes was said to have lived

schole, cultivated idleness, leisure

sophos, wise man

Acknowledgements

Big thanks to Robin Baird-Smith for commissioning this book, and to Octavia Stocker and Tomasz Hoskins at Bloomsbury Continuum for carrying it forward. Also thanks to Julian Mash, Sarah Head, Cathleen Bradford-McCormac and Fahmida Ahmed at Bloomsbury. To Graham Stocker for the copy editing. To Pamela Clemit for permission to use the William Godwin letters. To Victoria Hull for excellent suggestions. Finally massive thanks to Mark Vernon, my friend and teacher.

Index

Ad Helvium (Seneca) 180
Ad Marciam (Seneca) 179, 180
Ad Polybium (Seneca) 180
Agrippina, Emperor 8
Alcibiades
　dates for xiii
　description of xi
　and Socrates 14, 17, 20, 21, 22–5, 34, 38, 41, 45, 99
Alexander the Great xiii, 2, 101, 122
Ameipsias 154
Anatomy of Melancholy, The (Burton) 175
anger
　Christian view of 53–4
　and Diogenes Laertius 50–1
　and Epictetus 48, 49, 50, 51
　and Marcus Arelius 49
　and Seneca 48–9, 52
　Stoic view of 49–50, 51–3, 54–5
Annius Verus 10
Anthony, Marc 6, 69, 149, 186
Antoninus Pius 10
Anytus 23
Apology, The (Plato) 23, 68–9, 81–2, 123
Aristophanes 17
Aristotle xii, xiii
Arrianus, Flavius 9
Aspasia xi, xiii
Athens 14–16, 21–2, 165–6
Attalus the Stoic 7
Augustine, St
　dates for xiv
　description of xii
　and education 60
　and friendship 103–4
　influence of Stoicism on xvi
　and love 38, 39–40
　objections to Stoicism 153, 161
Aulus Gellius 20

Bakewell, Sarah 58
Beck, Aaron 192
Berlin, Isiah 190
Blake, William 196s
Boccaccio, Giovanni 59
Boétie, Etienne de la 97–9, 124
Boswell, James 79, 173
Buddha xiii, 139, 159, 194
Buddhism 47
Burton, Robert 175
Byron, Lord 34–5, 41

Caesar, Julius xiii, 5, 6, 146
Calendar of Wisdom, A (Tolstoy) 194
Caligula 7
Cassian, John xii, xiv, 43, 54
Cassius, Avidius 11–12
Cato the Elder xii, 138
Cato the Younger
　and Cicero 5
　and death 185
　description of xii
　and politics 72
Chaerophon 23
Chaucer, Geoffrey 8, 133, 195
cheerfulness
　and Charles Dickens 173–4
　and Chrysippus 175
　and Epictetus 176
　and Friedrich Nietzsche 176–7
　and Marcus Aurelius 175–6
　and Seneca 175
　and Socrates 175
　Stoic view of 174–5
　and Zeno of Citium 175
Christ xiii
Christianity
　and anger 53–4
　and happiness 87
　influence of Stoicism on 45–7, 48, 129–31, 192–4
　and mysticism 129–31
　and sin 45–7
Chrysippus
　and cheerfulness 175
　dates for xiii
　and death 186
　description of xii
　and fate 148
　and leisure 169
　life of 3–4
　and logic 108
Cicero
　dates for xiii
　and death 186
　description of xii
　and fate 144, 146–8
　legacy of 190
　and leisure 167–8
　life of 4–6
　and money 136
　and mysticism 129
　and pain 79–80, 82, 83, 84
　and politics 69–70, 71, 76
City of God (Augustine) 40, 161
Clairmont, Claire 34, 41
Claudius, Emperor 7
Cleanthes
　and Cicero 5
　description of xi
　and fate 145
　and mysticism 125, 126
Clodius xii, 6
Clouds, The (Aristophanes) 17
Cobian, Kurt 185
cognitive behavioural therapy (CBT) 191–2
Coleridge, Samuel Taylor 137
Commodus, Emperor 10, 12
'Comus' (Milton) 155–7
Confessions (Augustine) 60

INDEX

Confucius xiii
Consolatio (Cicero) 82
Crass 137
Crates the Cynic
  description of xi
  and development of
    Stoicism xv–xvi
  and leisure 167
  and love 40
  and Zeno of Citium 2
Cynics xvi

Dante 195
De Fato (Cicero) 6, 143, 144,
  146–8
De Otia (Seneca) 74
death
  and Cato the Younger 185
  and Charles Handy 184–5
  and Chrysippus 186
  and Cicero 186
  and Epictetus 187
  and Marcus Aurelius 183–4
  and Mary Shelley 179–80
  and Musonius Rufus 186
  and Seneca 179, 180–3, 186
  and Socrates 182
  and Zeno of Citium 185–6
Decameron (Boccaccio) 59
Democritus xi, 144
Dickens, Charles 52
Diodotus 4
Diogenes of Babylon xii
Diogenes the Cynic
  dates for xiii
  and development of
    Stoicism xv
  and education 64–5
  and freedom 118–19, 122
  and leisure 166
  and love 42
  and money 135
  and politics 73, 76
Diogenes Laertius
  and anger 50–1
  and Chrysippus 3–4
  description of xii
  and freedom 117
  and friendship 100
  and gluttony 53
  and happiness 90, 93
  and logic 107–8
  and love 36
  and money 135
  and mysticism 126, 129
  and politics 70
  and Socrates 13, 17, 21,
    30, 154
  and Zeno of Citium 2–3, 35,
    70, 185–6
Diogenes of Sinope xi, 94
Diognetus 10
Diotima 38

Discourses (Epictetus) 9, 37, 47,
  49, 50, 90, 151
Domitia Calivilla 10
Domitian, Emperor 9

education
  and Diogenes the Cynic 64–5
  and Epictetus 61–2
  and Marcus Aurelius 63
  and Mary Shelley 57–8
  and Michel de Montaigne
    58–9, 63, 65
  and Musonius Rufus 62
  and St Augustine 60
  and Seneca 61, 63–4
  Stoic view of 60–1, 62, 63, 64
Eleutheria 119–20
Eliot, T. S. 8, 46
Epaphroditus 9
Epictetus
  and anger 48, 49, 50, 51
  and cheerfulness 176
  and control of passions 47, 48
  dates for xiv
  and death 187
  description of xii
  and education 61–2
  and fate 145, 150–1
  and freedom 120–1
  and friendship 99–100
  and happiness 90, 91, 92, 93–4
  and leisure 171
  life of 8–9
  and logic 114
  and love 37–8, 40–1, 45
  and money 140
  and Musonius Rufus 7, 9
  and pain 78–9, 81, 85
  and politics 67, 76–7
Epicureans 144–5, 162–3,
  168–9, 193–4
Epicurus
  description of xii
  and mysticism 128
  and pain 78
Eubulides 108–9
Euripides 13
Evagrius Ponticus xii, xiv, 46, 47
Evans, Jules 191–2

Farrar, F. W. 11
fate
  and Chrysippus 148
  and Cicero 144, 146–8
  and Cleanthes 145
  and Epictetus 145, 150–1
  and Seneca 143, 149–50
  and Socrates 147
  Stoic view of 144, 145, 151–2
Faustina 10, 12
Ficino, Marsilio xviii
Foucault, Michel 121, 124
Frankenstein (Shelley) 58, 179

freedom
  and Diogenes the Cynic
    118–19, 122
  and Diogenes Laertius 117
  and Epictetus 120–1
  and Plato 119
  and slavery 117–18
  and Socrates 121, 123
  Stoic view of 118, 119–20,
    121–2, 124
  and Zeno of Citium 117
friendship
  and Diogenes Laertius 100
  and Epictetus 99–100
  and Marcus Aurelius 102–3
  and Michel de Montaigne
    97–9
  and St Augustine 103–4
  and Seneca 101–2
  and Socrates 99
  Stoic view of 97, 99–100
  and Zeno of Citium 97, 99
Fronto 10
Fulvia 6, 69

Gandhi, Mahatma 194
Gandhi and the Stoics
  (Sorabji) 194
'Garden, The' (Marvell) 75
Gay Science, The (Nietzsche) 162
gluttony 52–3
Goodwin, William 34, 57–8,
  179–80

Hadrian, Emperor 9, 10
Handbook (Epictetus) 9, 81
Handy, Charles 128, 184–5
happiness
  Christian view of 87
  and Diogenes Laertius 90, 93
  and Diogenes of Sinope 94
  and Epictetus 90, 91, 92, 93–4
  and objections to Stoicism
    161, 198–9
  and Seneca 87, 89, 93, 197
  and Socrates 94, 95
  Stoic view of 87–91, 92
Harries, Richard 130
Harris, Robert 163
harshness of Stoicism
  157–8, 198
Helen of Troy 101
Herennius 149
Herodes Atticus 10
Hesiod 31–2
Hipparchia
  description of xi
  and development of
    Stoicism xvi
  and love 40
  and Zeno of Citium 2
Horace 39
Huxley, Aldus 163

INDEX

Hymn to Zeus (Cleanthes) 125, 126

John, Elton 154–5
Johnson, Dr 79, 173
Julia 7
Jungle Book, The (film) 195

Keats, John 33

legacy of Stoicism xvi–xvii, xviii, 45–7, 189–96
leisure
  in Ancient Greece 165–6
  and Chrysippus 169
  and Cicero 167–8
  and Crates the Cynic 167
  and Diogenes the Cynic 166
  and Epictetus 171
  and Lucilius 170
  and Marcus Aurelius 170–1, 172
  and Pericles 166–7
  and Seneca 168–9, 170
  and Socrates 166
  Stoic view of 167
  and Zeno of Citium 167, 169
Lennon, John 89, 134, 155
'Letters on Ethics to Lucilius' (Seneca) 8
Life and Other Dangerous Situations (Evans) 191
Lloyd, John 159
Locke, John 61
logic
  and Chrysippus 108
  and Diogenes Laertius 107–8
  and Epictetus 114
  and Eubulides 108–9
  and Musonius Rufus 111–13
  and Seneca 111, 113
  and Socrates 113–14
  Stoic view of 109–10, 111, 113
  and Zeno of Citium 111
love
  and Crates the Cynic 40
  different forms of 31
  and Diogenes the Cynic 42
  and Diogenes Laertius 36
  and Epictetus 37–8, 40–1, 45
  and Hipparchia 40
  and Marcus Aurelius 39, 41–2
  and Plato 38
  and St Augustine 38, 39–40
  and Sappho 32–3, 38–9
  and Seneca 31, 36–7, 40
  and Socrates 31, 34, 36, 38–9, 45
  Stoic view of 33–4, 35–6, 40–3
  and Zeno of Citium 35
Love's Labours Lost (Shakespeare) 114

Lucilius
  description of xii
  and leisure 170
  and money 139
  and Seneca 40, 48–9, 63–4, 74, 78, 101, 133
Lucius 7
Lydon, John 54

Man in Full, A (Wolfe) xviii, 9, 190–1
manosphere 189–90
Marcia xii, 180–1
Marcus Aurelius
  and anger 49
  and cheerfulness 175–6
  dates for xiv
  and death 183–4
  description of xii
  and education 63
  and friendship 102–3
  and leisure 170–1, 172
  life of 10–12
  and love 39, 41–2
  and mysticism 130–2
Marley, Bob 118, 120
Martin Chuzzlewit (Dickens) 173–4
Marvell, Andrew 75
Marx, Karl 144–5
Maximus of Tyre 38–9
Medea xi, 83
Medea (Seneca) 8
Meditations (Marcus Aurelius) 10, 12, 49, 63, 131
Memorabilia (Xenophon) xv
Mill, John Stuart 12
Milton, John 152, 155–7
money
  and Cato the Elder 138
  and Cicero 136
  and Diogenes the Cynic 135
  and Diogenes Laertius 135
  and Epictetus 140
  and Lucilius 139
  and Musonius Rufus 136–7
  and objections to Stoicism 153–7
  and Seneca 133–4, 138, 139
  and Socrates 135, 153, 154
  Stoic view of 134–5, 136, 139–41
  and Zeno of Citium 135–6
  and Zenodutus the Stoic 133
Montaigne, Michel de xvi, 57, 58–9, 63, 65, 97–9, 124
More, Thomas 71
Mujica, José 138–9
Musk, Elon 123, 124
Musonius Rufus
  dates for xiii
  and death 186
  description of xii

  and education 62
  and Epictetus 7, 9
  life of 7
  and logic 111–13
  and money 136–7
mysticism
  Christian view of 129–31
  and Cicero 129
  and Cleanthes 125, 126
  and Diogenes Laertius 126, 129
  and Epicurus 128
  and Marcus Aurelius 130–2
  and oracle of Delphi 129
  and Socrates 132
  Stoic view of 125, 126–8, 129–30

Nero xii, xiii, 8, 186
Nietzsche, Friedrich 162–3, 176–7

objections to Stoicism
  and Elton John 154–5
  and Friedrich Nietzsche 162–3
  and happiness 161, 198–9
  harshness of Stoicism 157–8, 198
  and John Milton 155–7
  lack of passion 162–3
  and money 153–7
  perfectionism of Stoicism 158–60
  and St Augustine 153, 161
  sterility of Stoicism 160–1
Octavia xii
'On Friendship' (Montaigne) 98–9
'On Mercy' (Seneca) 157–8
'On Providence' (Seneca) 143, 149
Ono, Yoko 155
oracle of Delphi 16, 125, 129
Origen 7
Ovid xii, 67

P Diddy Combs 138
pain
  and Cicero 79–80, 82, 83, 84
  and Epictetus 78–9, 81, 85
  and Epicurus 78
  and Plato 81–2
  and Seneca 77, 78
  and Socrates 81–2, 83
  Stoic view of 77–8, 80–1, 82, 85
Paradise Lost (Milton) 152
Paradoxa Stoicorum (Cicero) 5
passions
  control of 47–8
  as objection to Stoicism 162–3
Paul, St xiii, xvi, 129–30, 192, 193–4

INDEX

Paulina 186
perfectionism of Stoicism 158–60
Pericles
  dates for xiii
  description of xi
  and leisure 166–7
  sexuality of 22
Phaedrus 4, 39
Phaedrus (Plato) 182
Phaenarete 16
Philo 4
Philokalia, The 46
Phrynne 22
Plato
  dates for xiii
  description of xii
  and freedom 119
  and love 38
  and pain 81–2
  and politics 68–9
  and Socrates 13, 22, 23, 27
Plutarch
  and Cicero 143
  description of xii
  and politics 70–1
  and Socrates 14, 19, 27
politics
  and Cato the Younger 72
  and Cicero 69–70, 71, 76
  and Diogenes the Cynic 73, 76
  and Diogenes Laertius 70
  and Epictetus 67, 76–7
  involvement of 72–3
  meanings of 67–8
  and Ovid 67
  and Plato 68–9
  and Plutarch 70–1
  and reputations 76
  and Seneca 73–5
  and Socrates 68–9
  truth in 69
  and Zeno of Citium 70–1, 74
Posidonius the Stoic 5, 110
Publilia 5, 143
Pythagoras xi, 129

Regulus, Marcus 6
Republic, The (Plato) 36, 71

Sackler family 80–1
Sappho xi, 32–3, 38–9
Satires (Horace) 39
Self-Help (Smiles) 190
Seneca
  and anger 48–9, 52
  and cheerfulness 175
  dates for xiii
  and death 179, 180–3, 186
  description of xii
  and education 61, 63–4
  and fate 143, 149–50
  and friendship 101–2

and gluttony 53
and happiness 87, 89, 93, 197
influence of 8
legacy of 190, 192, 195
and leisure 168–9, 170
life of 7–8
and logic 111, 113
and love 31, 36–7, 40
and money 133–4, 138, 139
and Musonius Rufus 7
and objections to Stoicism 157–9
and pain 77, 78
and politics 73–5
Seuren, Pieter A. M. 109
Shakespeare, William xvi, 114
Shelley, Mary 34, 57–8
Shelley, Percy 34
Sherman, Nancy 190
sin 45–7
Smiles, Samuel 190
Socrates
  and Alcibiades 14, 17, 20, 21, 22–5, 34, 38, 41, 45, 99
  and cheerfulness 175
  dates for xiii
  and death 182
  description of xi
  and education 64, 65
  and fate 147
  and freedom 121, 123
  and friendship 99
  and happiness 94, 95
  and leisure 166
  life of 13–14, 16–21, 22–30
  and logic 113–14
  and love 31, 34, 36, 38–9, 45
  and money 135, 153, 154
  and mysticism 132
  and pain 81–2, 83
  and politics 68–9
  toughness of 61
Some Thoughts Concerning Education (Locke) 61
Sophroniscus 16
Sorabji, Richard 194
Southey, Robert 137
Standing, Guy 72–3
Statius Prisicius 11
sterility of Stoicism 160–1
Stockdale, Admiral 80, 190
Stoic Wisdom: Ancient Lessons in Modern Resilience (Sherman) 190
Stoicism
  and anger 49–50, 51–3, 54–5
  and cheerfulness 174–5
  and Christianity 45–7, 48, 129–31, 192–4
  control of passions in 47–8
  development of xv–xviii
  and education 60–1, 62, 63, 64

and fate 144, 145, 151–2
and freedom 118, 119–20, 121–2, 124
and friendship 97, 99–100
and gluttony 52–3
and happiness 87–91, 92
legacy of xvi–xvii, xviii, 45–7, 189–96
and logic 109–10, 111, 113
and love 33–4, 35–6, 40–3
and mysticism 125, 126–8, 129–30
objections to 153–63
and pain 77–8, 80–1, 82, 85
self-knowledge in 17
Symposium (Plato) 22, 38

Tale of Melibee (Chaucer) 8, 195
Terentia 5
That One Should Learn to Disdain Hardship (Musonius Rufus) 7
Theogony (Hesiod) 31–2
Thunberg, Greta 122
Tolstoy, Leo 1, 8, 12, 45, 194, 197
Tullia 5, 82, 143, 149
Tusculan Disputations (Cicero) 5, 79, 167–8
'Two Concepts of Liberty' (Berlin) 190

Uncommercial Traveller, The (Dickens) 52

Vernon, Mark 192
Verus, Lucius 10, 11

Williams, Rowan 43, 47, 53, 130, 160–1
Wilson, Emily 133–4, 186
Wolfe, Tom xviii, 9, 190–1
Wollstonecraft, Mary 58

Xanthippe xi, 19–20, 39, 175
Xenophon xv, 13, 23

Zeno of Citium
  and cheerfulness 175
  dates for xiii
  and death 185–6
  description of xi
  and development of Stoicism xv–xvi, xvii
  and freedom 117
  and friendship 97, 99
  and leisure 167, 169
  life of 2–3
  and logic 111
  and love 35
  and money 135–6
  and politics 70–1, 74
Zenodutus the Stoic xii, 133